KU-709-400

WITHDRAWN

KU-709-400

# sound
# design

## classic audio
## & hi-fi design

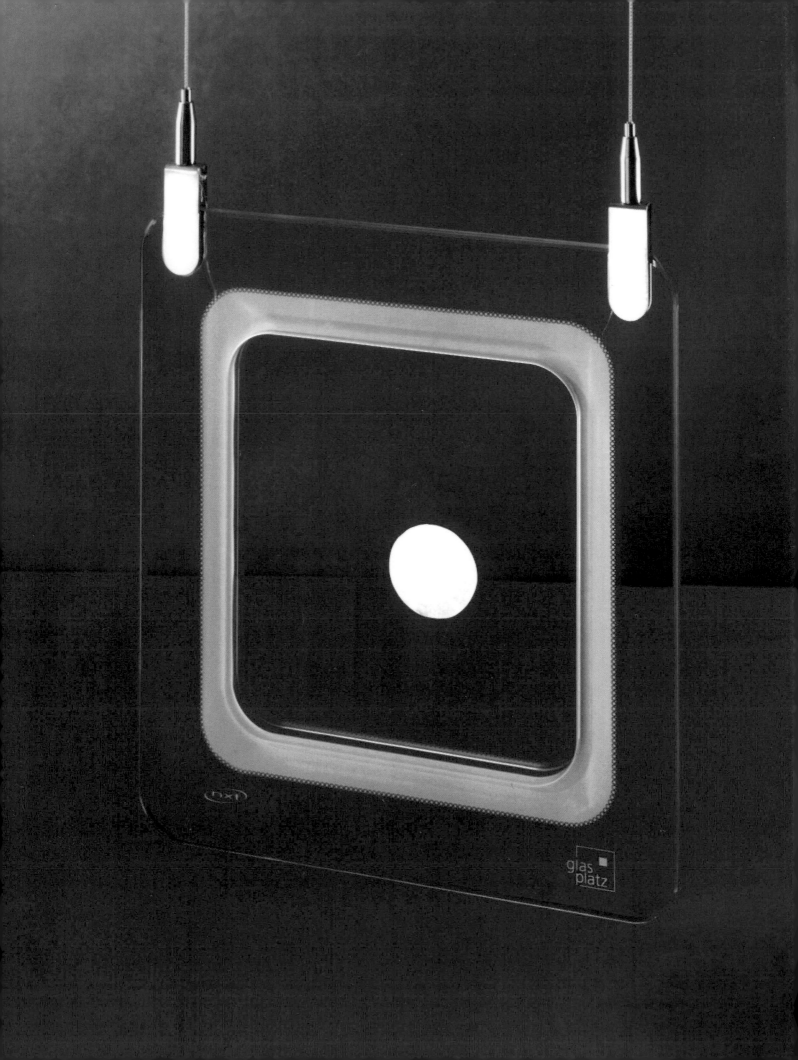

# sound
# design

## classic audio
## & hi-fi design

U.W.E.L.
LEARNING RESOURCES

ACC. No.
2285521

CLASS
621.
3893
ATT

CONTROL
1840005068

DATE
-2. DEC 2002

SITE
WV

**David Attwood**

# SOU

**David At**

Copyright

First publi
an imprint
2-4 Herol

Commissi
Executive
Executive
Project Ec
Editor **Pe**
Designer
Productio
Picture R
Indexer **/**

A CIP cat
available

ISBN 1 8

All rights
or utilized
including
and retrie

Set in Eu
Produced
Printed a

▲ The Philco Transitone radio's
boomerang shape and pastel colouring
are typical of the early 1950s.

1945-1959 **radio**culture

## SONY TR610

In 1953 a young Japanese company, then called Tokyo Communications, got a licence from AT&T to make transistor chips, and two years later launched its first transistor radio in Japan, the Sony TR55. It was about the same size as the Emerson 838 (see p.13), and it was followed in 1957 by the TR63 and then other shirt-pocket Sonys, which all sold well in the US and Europe. Of these, the TR610 is the best known – nearly half a million sets were sold – and the edge controls, handle, and trim set a trend for countless other pocket sets. Typically, the TR610's six transistors are promoted on the front, but, in addition, much work went into miniaturizing the set's other components.

48                                    Electrical and Radio Trading. January 7, 1956

The "Lady Margaret" market is still

# EXPANDING!

EVERY NEW T.V. SET
•
EVERY NEW CARAVAN
•
EVERY NEW
HOLIDAY CAMP BOOKING

means trade for YOU!

# VIDOR "LADY MARGARET"
## DOMINANT IN PORTABLES

VIDOR · LIMITED · ERITH · KENT

▶

date of introduction: **1958, Japan**

size: **10 x 6 x 2 cm (4 x 2¼ x ¾ in)**

key features: **best-selling pocket set; trend-setting styling**

▲ In the 1950s the "vanity case" became a popular style for radios targeted at women.

they were almost twice the price. However, between 1957 and 1959, as prices fell and pop music exploded into public consciousness, transistor portables surged in popularity. In radios, as in Sir Alec Issigonis's ground-breaking car design, "mini"-sized products were now the fashion.

## New materials, styles, and brands

The 1950s brought new materials such as polystyrene, which was lighter than previous plastics and could be moulded in a wide range of colours.

As sales of radios levelled off, makers had to find ways of selling the public a second set. Electro-mechanical clock radios sold well for a time, while, in an early example of targeted marketing, portables styled to look like vanity cases were promoted to women as a fashion accessory (see left). As the age of the transistor dawned, lunch-box-sized portable sets were cased in plastic or leatherette, often with a choice of colour schemes or "polka-dot" patterns typical of the 1950s. The word "transistor" was often picked out in gold as a symbol of modernity.

After the war Japan had had to rebuild its economy, and early Japanese exports had a poor image. But in 1955 a young Tokyo company launched its first transistor radio in Japan. Its brand name, Sony, would come to dominate the technological and cultural landscape of the late twentieth century. Small pocket sets from Sony (see p.14) and ▶▶

## ROBERTS RT1

Founded in 1932, Roberts quickly established a reputation for solidly made portable radios. The RT1 was the company's first transistor model, but followed the company tradition of using a handmade wooden cabinet covered in leather cloth. The set came in several plain colours as well as this polka-dot pattern that was typical of the 1950s. Roberts artfully promoted transistor radios as glamorous fashion accessories; celebrities of the time were photographed holding one-offs that were clad in mink, leopard-skin, and even solid gold. The traditional look has kept the Roberts brand alive while other 1950s setmakers have been forgotten, and the company currently has "Revival" models on sale which have retro-styling that is almost identical to the classic RT1.

◀

date of introduction: **1959, UK**

size: **17 x 25 x 11 cm (6³/₄ x 9³/₄ x 4¹/₄ in)**

key features: **wooden cabinet; timeless "British" look**

other Japanese firms soon followed. Within a few years these brands would have a devastating effect on the West's radio industry.

## The growth of FM

The AM frequency had one big problem: it suffered from fading and interference. Edwin Armstrong had first demonstrated "frequency modulation" (FM), in 1933, but it was not until after the Second World War that FM was relaunched on its present frequency band. Most big US cities had a choice of specialized music stations by the mid '50s, while listeners in the UK had to wait until 1954 for the BBC to start transmitting on FM (or VHF as it was called then).

But FM was slow to take off. While classical music and hi-fi enthusiasts valued its silent background and extended treble range, these benefits were also on offer from the new long-playing records. And many listeners were quite happy with AM – they just wanted a better choice of music. Few portable radios had FM until around 1960. However, the arrival of FM and the LP did strengthen the market for larger table radios and radiogram consoles.

## New speeds for records

While a 78rpm disc that was in mint condition gave quite good sound quality, the steel or fibre needles quickly wore the grooves, raising noise levels. This, plus the short playing time (only six minutes for a twelve-inch

### MOTOROLA 56TI

This was Motorola's first transistor model, produced in 1955, at a time when most makers still had both tube and transistor portables in their ranges. Early transistor radios were significantly more expensive and sometimes had poorer performance than tube models. Nevertheless the presence of the wonder technology is prominently advertised on the handle. The stylized loudspeaker grille is typical of the way designers sought to make their products stand out, often borrowing chevrons and other trim details from 1950s automobiles.

▶

date of introduction: **1955, US**

size: **9 x 14 x 4cm (3¹/₂ x 5¹/₂ x 1¹/₂in)**

key features: **early transistor model; metal case; handle antenna**

## MURPHY A242R

Since the mid-1930s Murphy had employed furniture designer Dick Russell (of the Gordon Russell furniture company) to give its wooden cabinets a simple modern look, which at first shocked those with more traditional tastes. These standards persisted into the 1940s and early '50s with the innovative use of bakelite and wood by in-house designers such as A.F. Thwaites. The A242R radiogram appeared just as VHF (FM) radio was launched in the UK and LP record sales were beginning to take off: Murphy's first AM/FM radio chassis was combined with a three-speed Garrard record-changer. The furniture style is discreet by 1950s standards, but the high-gloss veneer is typical of the decade.

▲

date of introduction: **1955, UK**

size: **96.5 x 99 x 40.5 cm (38 x 39 x 16 in)**

key features: **four-band AM/FM radio; three-speed record player**

(30cm) 78 side) meant there was little interest in obtaining high-quality sound from discs. However, after 1945, both Columbia (CBS) and RCA developed new and competing $33\frac{1}{3}$ and 45 rpm record technologies, which used lightweight vinyl instead of the brittle shellac used for 78s (see p.19). In the UK, the Decca company introduced LPs in 1950. Decca (known as "London" in the US) was already ahead in sound quality, having introduced "ffrr" (full frequency range recording), which greatly extended the recorded bass and treble frequency range of 78s. The other big British record company, EMI, was slower off the mark, persisting for several years in producing 78 rpm records and players only. ▶▶

# ALL AMERICA'S TALKING ABOUT RCA VICTOR'S AMAZING NEW 45 RPM SYSTEM

**First record and changer ever designed to work together . . .**

## YOU WON'T BELIEVE YOUR EYES!

A system streamlined in size and cost, thrilling in performance! A tiny translucent record only 7 inches across that can play more than 5 minutes on a side! An astonishing new changer that works from *inside* the spindle . . . changes *noiselessly, instantaneously* . . . plays as many as ten sides with only one touch of a button! And it plays anything you select, for all types of music are now on the same size records. They all fit into your ordinary bookcase shelf . . . 18 albums or nearly 150 single records to the foot!

## YOU WON'T BELIEVE YOUR EARS!

Now, for the first time, you hear true "live-talent" quality on records! As the diagram shows, all records can have a "quality zone" where music is undistorted. But toward the center is a "distortion zone" where music loses clarity and brilliance. Now, however, a new speed, size, pickup and groove-system are all combined in the new 45 rpm records to place *all* the music in the distortion-free "quality zone." This has *never* been achieved before— never before such clarity, depth and brilliance on records! *And there is virtually no surface noise!*

All music recorded in the "quality zone"

## NOW...FIRST TRUE "LIVE-TALENT" QUALITY!

. . . and all you need to enjoy it through your present set is this tiny plug-in player. Has *world's fastest changer.* Many find it fits right into their desk drawer or console storage compartment. With improved "Silent Sapphire" permanent-point jewel pickup. Deep maroon plastic cabinet. The RCA Victor 9-JY. AC. Only **$24.95***

**Less than 10 inches square** . . . a complete phonograph with unbelievably full tone and volume! Handy to move from room to room. New pickup is *3 times lighter*—only ⅓ ounce pressure on records. Maroon cabinet. The 9-EY-3. AC. **$39.95***

**A masterpiece of compactness** with two record changers . . . for your present records, *and* your new, finer 45 rpm collection! Room for 18 new albums plus 20 conventional albums. Finished in mahogany or walnut. (Modern blond slightly more.) It's the RCA Victor 9-W-105. AC. **$269.50***

## YOU WON'T BELIEVE THE PRICE!

Only 95¢* for the new Red Seal records! Only 65¢* for all others! Improved, simpler changer-design has brought instrument prices down, too. *More* economy: the new non-breakable Vinylite records actually wear up to 10 times longer than conventional records. Unique "surface-saver" shoulders protect the playing surfaces while records are stacked or stored away. Playing surfaces don't touch. *Truly—better music for more people at low cost!*

| Red Seal Records | 95¢* |
|---|---|
| All Others Only | 65¢* |

## QUICK COLOR IDENTIFICATION!

It's a unique new "easy identification" system! A different color for each type of music makes records easier to select and store away . . . more fun to play. *They all fit in ordinary bookshelves.* A superb collection of all-time favorites is now ready to choose from at your dealer's, and now the *new releases, too!*

CLASSICAL · POPULAR · COUNTRY AND WESTERN · CHILDREN'S · POPULAR-CLASSICS · BLUES AND RHYTHM · INTERNATIONAL

"78's" too! If you own a conventional player you can still enjoy a full selection of RCA Victor recordings. *All new releases, Red Seal and popular, will also be issued for the 78 rpm system.*

*All prices shown are subject to change without notice. Record prices do not include Federal Excise or local taxes.

# RCA VICTOR

DIVISION OF RADIO CORPORATION OF AMERICA

**WORLD LEADER IN RADIO . . . FIRST IN RECORDED MUSIC . . . FIRST IN TELEVISION**

## COMPETING SPEEDS

In the late 1940s new, competing record technologies were launched in the US which used lightweight vinyl instead of the brittle shellac used for 78s. Columbia was first with 33⅓rpm discs in 1948, though in fact this speed had been used for cinema soundtrack discs since the 1930s. The fine "microgrooves" gave a quiet background and up to about twenty-five minutes play per side. RCA's seven-inch (18cm) 45rpm disc lasted just over five minutes; its large centre hole fitted the special changer designed for it. At first consumers were confused by the speeds war, but, in the end, both speeds succeeded, with 33⅓rpm being used for LPs and 45rpm discs replacing 78s to become the standard pop single format for the next twenty-five years.

◄ RCA's 45rpm discs had a large centre hole – a "spider" or adaptor was needed to fit the disc to a standard spindle.

► Columbia's 33⅓ discs at first came in three sizes but triumphed in the ten-inch and twelve-inch LP format.

"Now stack up those 7-inch 33⅓ Lp pops 12 HITS HIGH!"

says NELSON EDDY
Exclusive Columbia Records Artist

**From the world's largest Catalog of 33⅓ LP Records** which you can play automatically on the Model 104 Columbia LP Changer Attachment

**7-INCH**

FRANK SINATRA — "American Beauty Rose" and "Just An Old Stone House" 7-inch LP 1-624

DINAH SHORE — "Simple Melody" and "I Still Get A Thrill" 7-inch LP 1-656

PERCY FAITH — with Russ Emery, vocal "I Cross My Fingers" and "Valencia" 7-inch LP 1-607

NELSON EDDY — Schubert: Serenade and Schubert: Ave Maria 7-inch LP 3-529

**10-INCH**

Naughty Marietta 8 selections sung by Nelson Eddy and Nadine Conner with chorus and orchestra conducted by Robert Armbruster. ML 2094

DANCE DATES A brand-new series of 33⅓ LP Records especially designed for your dancing pleasure. Two complete dance sets on each record . . . exactly as you would dance to them in the ballroom. Good for listening, too! Your favorite dance tunes played by these favorite artists.
Your Dance Date with Xavier Cugat CL 6121
Your Dance Date with Les Brown CL 6123
Your Dance Date with Tony Pastor CL 6122
Your Dance Date with Hal McIntyre CL 6124

**12-INCH**

NELSON EDDY "Songs of Stephen Foster". Nelson Eddy sings 21 of your favorite Stephen Foster melodies . . . Chorus and orchestra conducted by Robert Armbruster. ML 4099

KOSTELANETZ—Swan Lake Ballet Music (Tchaikovsky) Andre Kostelanetz and His Orchestra. ML 4308

NEW COLUMBIA Lp CHANGER ATTACHMENT MODEL 104 $16.95

Plays All Sizes and Makes of 33⅓ LP Records Automatically! A $32.95 value for only

Playing records is all play and no work with the new Columbia LP Changer. It automatically handles twelve of the hit-size 7-inch 33⅓ LP records, or twelve 10-inch, or ten 12-inch Long Playing records with one loading. Hear hours of music with one touch of the button! This one-speed player is all you need to enjoy every kind of recorded music—popular and classical—with the matchless brilliance, convenience and economy of the Columbia 33⅓ LP system. It's wonderful! Easily attached to any radio or television set. See it at your dealer's now.

## COLUMBIA Lp RECORDS

33⅓ LP ONE SPEED IS ALL YOU NEED

"Columbia," "Masterworks," ⓡ and ⓒ Trade Marks Reg. U. S. Pat. Of. Marcas Registradas

In the end, both new speeds succeeded, with Columbia selling 45s and RCA selling 33s by 1951 (see "Competing Speeds", above left).

### The radiogram and the record player

In the 1930s those who could afford them could buy expensive and elaborate radios built into floor-standing wooden cabinets. It was a fairly simple step to add an electric turntable and pick-up to this, and the result was a console or "radiogram" – a piece of furniture that persisted in some form or other well into the 1960s. The short playing time of 78s had made automatic record-changers popular and, in the pre-LP era, long classical recordings came in "auto couplings", where ten "side ones" could be played before the whole stack needed to be turned over.

Few people in the late '40s and early '50s owned portable electric record players. Some bought an electric turntable and pick-up to plug into their table radio. However, the new 33⅓ and 45rpm records ►►

◀ Radio on the move: this convertible model appealed to teenagers because it could slot into the car dashboard or be used on its own as a small portable.

# radios for all

In the late 1940s most home entertainment still derived from the radio, but as television's evening menu of variety, quiz shows, and sitcoms caught on, the TV set enjoyed pride of place in the living room. Radio took a back seat as a source of news and music, and family members started listening individually in different rooms around the house. Setmakers soon realized that this was a way to sell more radios and launched sets which were specially styled to appeal to women. Then, as radio stations latched on to rock'n'roll and pop in the late '50s, teenagers urgently needed their own space and their own radio.

People also listened more to radio in their cars, and demand for drive-time music, news, and traffic reports helped to keep the medium alive. In the following decades car audio would become a huge industry in its own right.

Small pocket radios had been talked about for a long time, but the late '40s and early '50s were not the time to market them. Post-war consumers wanted everything big – a large new TV made a much better status symbol than a miniaturized radio. A few "personal" valve sets were made but were mostly dismissed as toys or gimmicks, while earphones – so stylish thirty years later with a Walkman cassette player – back in the 1950s looked too much like a hearing aid for comfort.

Ten years later, though, a small earpiece plugged into a transistor portable offered teenagers a blissful escape to a world of girl groups, early Motown, and the Beatles. Radios were no longer dusty wooden boxes stuck in stuffy living rooms, but cherished, go-anywhere fashion accessories.

▲ Some portable battery-operated record players, like this Dansette, included a radio too.

◄ A selection of KB transistor radios from the end of the 1950s.

stimulated sales of record players and radiograms. Three-speed players had pick-ups with separate plug-in heads or flipover cartridges with sapphire or diamond styluses for both 78 and microgroove discs. As sales of 45rpm pop singles took off in the late '50s, the musical tastes of teenagers and their parents were more at odds than ever, and small portable record players became hugely popular.

## The "furniture" look

In 1950s America, TV and audio equipment reached new heights of luxury. In the UK, too, a reaction to war-time shortages made the opulence and familiarity of traditional furniture styles popular for radios and radiograms. But the 1951 Festival of Britain popularized a lighter "contemporary" style, though some aspects of this – such as cocktail-cabinet styles – became 1950s design clichés (see p.36).

In Britain the Council of Industrial Design promoted a simple, modern, rather Scandinavian aesthetic. The Council was well-meaning but often patronizing: "Are people who buy radiograms really as lacking in taste as all that?" it asked in 1960. Such design pundits argued for a central role for the industrial designer in the production process, and were against design as "styling" to be stuck on as an afterthought. In fact, radiograms persisted into the stereo era, representing the tension between the urge to hide technology within reassuring furniture styles, and the wish to highlight its modernity with a "scientific" look.

Simple modern design was easier to find elsewhere. In the US, ▶▶

### DANSETTE PORTABLE RECORD PLAYER

In the late 1940s Margolin, a small British company, sold a record-playing adaptor that plugged into a table radio. Then, at the suggestion of BSR, a maker of low-cost record-changers, the company went on to produce portable players with the name "Dansette". These were fairly basic, but became hugely popular as sales of 45rpm pop singles took off in the late '50s. Teenagers loved the Dansette's "smart two-tone styling" and go-anywhere portability, which contrasted with the dowdy radiograms in their parents' living rooms. Though long disused, the brand name is still powerfully evocative of late '50s British pop culture.

▶

date of introduction: **c.1960, UK**

size: **50 x 40 x 25 cm (19¹/₂ x 15³/₄ x 10 in)**

key features: **four-speed record changer; radio (on model shown); choice of colours**

**Admiral *triple thrill!***

TWO-SPEED PHONOGRAPH...MAGIC MIRROR TELEVISION...FM-AM RADIO

*America's Smart Set*

ADMIRAL TELEVISION CONSOLES
WITH MATCHING
RADIO-PHONOGRAPHS

**ABOVE**—Magic Mirror Television, 10" picture screen. Modern or traditional console. Walnut. **$299.95**

**LEFT**—New two-speed automatic radio-phonographs in matching consoles as low as **$169.95**

**3-Way Portable**
Plays instantly on AC or DC, as well as batteries. Beautiful emperor red and French gold case. **$34.95**

**FM-AM Radio and Automatic Phonograph**
Costs little more than an FM-AM radio alone! Plays up to 12 records automatically with Miracle tone arm. Mahogany **$99.95**

*Prices slightly higher in far south*

## *Complete Home Entertainment all in One Luxurious Console* $499.95
walnut

From Admiral comes *complete* home entertainment to charm your family and guests. Magic Mirror Television brings you bright, steady, mirror-like pictures on a big 10" direct view screen . . . the clearest pictures of them all!

Super-powered by 29 tubes to assure dependable performance even in out-lying areas. New two-speed automatic phonograph plays standard as well as new LP (long play) 45 minute microgroove records. Here, too, is a powerful radio with the finest features in FM-AM as developed by Admiral.

Truly a triple thrill . . . all combined in a breath-takingly beautiful cabinet that measures just 48 inches wide! See it! Hear it! Today!

*Installation and one year's service contract extra. Federal tax $5.25.*

◄ In the early 1950s combination consoles like this one symbolized luxury. Unfortunately they were at odds with the different ways TV and audio were used.

▼

date of introduction: **1954, UK**

size: **43 x 35 x 28 cm (17 x 13³/4 x 11in)**

key features: **good-quality amplifier; twin speakers**

## PYE BLACK BOX

This version of the Pye Black Box was decorated in Chinese lacquer and would, as *The Gramophone* magazine remarked in 1954, "grace any drawing room or boudoir". More often sold in humbler wood veneers, the Black Box was still a better than average record player, with a twin (though mono) speaker system in a well-designed cabinet. Pye of Cambridge, which had played a big part in the history of the British radio industry since the 1920s, was one of the first such companies to grasp the significance of the hi-fi revolution, and introduced ranges of hi-fi amplifier separates in the mid 1950s, as well as more conventional record players and radiograms.

date of introduction: **1956, Germany**

designers: **Hans Gugelot, Dieter Rams**

size: **58 x 29 x 24 cm (22³/₄ x 11¹/₂ x 9¹/₂ in)**

key features: **transparent lid; simple construction**

## BRAUN SK4 PHONOSUPER

The Braun company goes back to 1921 but its fame dates from the 1950s, when designers from the Ulm design school were brought in to rethink its range. Hans Gugelot (1920–65) joined Braun in 1954, to be followed a year later by former architect Dieter Rams (b.1932). Together they developed a sleek, unornamented look which became synonymous with Braun. The transparent plastic lid for the Phonosuper led to the nickname "Snow White's coffin", but the concept was widely taken up by the developing hi-fi industry in the 1960s. The one-piece metal casing framed by two wooden sides was also typical of their elegant engineering economy.

for example, George Nelson's cleanly styled storage designs for Herman Miller often included provision for building in audio/TV equipment (see right). The restrained functionalism of radios and radiograms produced by the German company Braun was a minority taste at the time, but as hi-fi entered the mainstream in the 1960s, this rational aesthetic combined with Japanese high-quality mass-production techniques to produce a more or less international high-tech style for audio equipment.

### Getting it taped

Ways of recording sound on steel wire or tape had been patented since the turn of the century. German companies pioneered recording on coated plastic tape, with BASF and AEG demonstrating the Magnetophon at the Berlin World Fair in 1935. After the Second World War some of these machines were taken to the US, and the 3M and Ampex companies started work on developing tapes and recorders. They produced their first professional machines in 1948, and disc masters as well as radio programmes were soon being pre-recorded on to tape.

In the same year, Willi Studer started Revox, the company that would become renowned in the world's recording studios for tape-recording and mixing equipment, as well as the equally legendary Revox tape ▶▶

## GEORGE NELSON FURNITURE

George Nelson (1908–86) was one of the most influential figures in modern furniture design. In his 1945 book *Tomorrow's House,* he focused on how modernist design concepts such as wall storage units and room dividers could be incorporated into American homes. His designs for the furniture company Herman Miller (above), consisting of a series of modular sectional units, look conventional enough in our flat-pack, knock-down age, but at the time they were revolutionary. They were ideally suited to a less formal era, and for installing the TVs and audio separates that modern homeowners wished to display rather than conceal.

▲

date of introduction: **1950s, US**

key features: **modernist design; flexible layout**

▼ A British coffee-table hi-fi enclosure with a contemporary 1950s look. In the search for domestically acceptable ways to present hi-fi equipment, some designers briefly resorted to disguising them as coffee tables.

machines for top-end amateur use (see right). Professional portable tape-recorders like the Nagra and the Uher were also widely used by broadcasters on location, while from the late '50s tape cartridge machines brought new slickness to radio stations' output.

The 1950s saw rapid growth in tape-recording. As well as Revox and Ampex, brands like Ferrograph catered for the top end of the market, while Philips, Grundig, and Wollensak (see below) supplied more modestly priced models. In the mid '50s EMI in the UK and RCA Victor in the US launched pre-recorded music tapes, but these failed to sell well. There were too few titles, and tape-threading was too awkward. From 1958 consumers went for stereo discs instead. But for a time tape-recording remained a popular hobby – many experimented with sound effects or editing, for example – and some later went on to work in professional studios. Several manufacturers, including RCA and Garrard, developed pre-loaded tape systems to make tape easier to use, but mass acceptance of tape came only with Philips's compact cassette in the '60s.

## The birth of hi-fi

The limitations of 78s and AM radio had meant that there was little to gain by improving home audio equipment. Even after the advent of FM and the LP, "high fidelity" was a hobby for the devoted few until the late '50s. Hi-fi's early days were linked to the need for high-power sound in theatres and cinemas and professional designs often found their way into the ▶▶

## WOLLENSAK T1515-4

A portable tape recorder by Wollensak of Chicago which ran on into the 1960s with transistors eventually replacing the original tube circuitry. Quarter-track machines like this one offered extra value from expensive recording tape by fitting four mono tracks (or two sets of stereo tracks) onto the quarter-inch wide medium. This model was wired for stereo playback and a matching amplifier/speaker unit was available. Two tape speeds were provided along with pushbutton operation and a "rev counter" to aid programme location. In the '70s Wollensak went on to produce high quality cassette decks.

▶

date of introduction: **1958, US**

size: **30 x 26 x 16.5cm**
**(11³/₄ x 10¹/₄ x 6¹/₂ in)**

key features: **quarter track; simple controls**

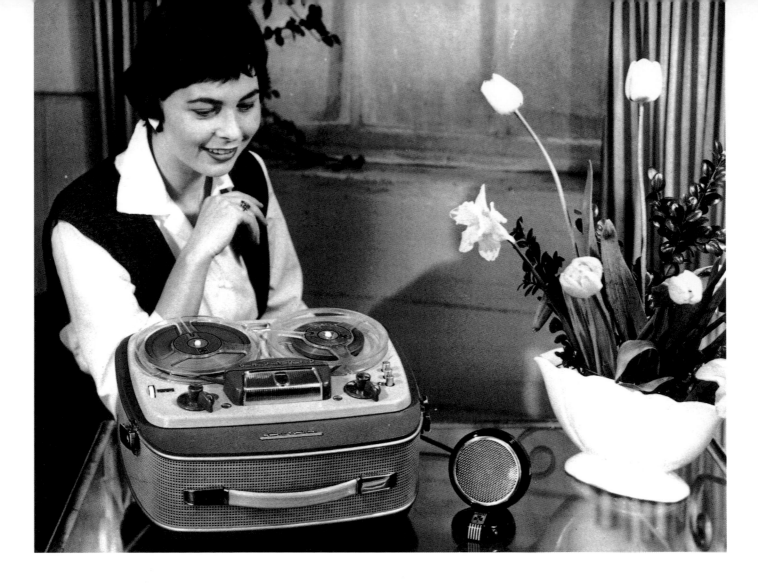

## REVOX 36 SERIES

Studer grew famous for studio-recording equipment, but its Revox machines for amateur use were equally renowned, especially the series which ran from the A36 in 1956 through to the G36 (shown here) in the early '60s. Styling and controls remained quite similar throughout, though early models had a green "magic eye" instead of meters to check recording level and, later, stereo and mixing facilities were added. Solenoid-controlled push-button operation gave quick start-up. The G36 was widely used by musicians (the first Rolling Stones album was reputedly mastered on one), as was the later Revox A77 model (1967).

▲ The Grundig TK24: a neat quarter-track model from a name synonymous with home tape recording in the '50s and '60s

▼

date of introduction: **1956, Switzerland**

designer: **Willi Studer**

size: **47 x 28 x 35.5 cm (18¹/₂ x 11 x 14 in)**

key features: **three motors; separate record and play circuits**

▲

date of introduction: **1949, UK**

designer: **Harold Leak**

size: **25.5 x 31.5 x 20.5cm (10 x 12½ x 8in)**

key features: **twelve watts output; less than 0.1 per cent distortion**

▼ The Heath company had made aircraft parts since the 1920s but from the late '40s pioneered high-quality kits for electronics enthusiasts.

## LEAK POINT ONE TL12

After the TL12 amplifier was shown at the New York Audio Fair in 1949, Leak, from its west London factory became one of the most successful UK audio exporters. Using the negative feedback circuit technique to reduce distortion, the TL12 was impeccably constructed and hand-wired with high-quality "tropicalized" components. It became widely used by broadcasters throughout the world. Typical of many amplifiers of the time, its large transformers were set alongside the valves on the steel chassis, which was stove-enamelled in bronze or gold. It cost just under £26 and is one of the many Leak designs prized by collectors today. A pre-amplifier/control unit was also available.

HEATHKIT
*High Fidelity*
"BUILD IT YOURSELF"
amplifier kits

*Build it*
YOURSELF

*Heathkit*
WILLIAMSON TYPE
(ACROSOUND TRANSFORMER)
This dual-chassis high fidelity amplifier kit provides installation flexibility. It features the Acrosound "ultra-linear" output transformer, and has a frequency response within 1 db from 10 cps to 100,000 cps. Harmonic distortion and intermodulation distortion are less than .5% at 5 watts, and maximum power output is well over 20 watts. A truly outstanding performer. W-3M consists of main amplifier and power supply. Shpg. Wt. 29 lbs., Express only ........................ **$49.75**
Model W-3 consists of W-3M plus WA-P2 Preamplifier listed on this page. Shpg. Wt. 37 lbs., Express only ........................ **$69.50**

*Heathkit*
HIGH FIDELITY PREAMPLIFIER
MODEL WA-P2

Here is the complete preamplifier. Designed specifically for use with the Williamson Type circuit, it provides equalization for LP, RIAA, AES, and early 78 records, 5 switch-selected inputs with individually preset level controls, separate bass and treble tone controls, special hum control, etc. Outstanding in performance and most attractive in appearance. Fulfills every requirement for true high fidelity performance. Shpg. Wt. 7 lbs. ........................ **$19.75**

*Heathkit*
WILLIAMSON TYPE
(CHICAGO TRANSFORMER)
This hi-fi amplifier is constructed on a single chassis, thereby affecting a reduction in cost. Uses new Chicago high fidelity output transformer and provides the same high performance as Model W-3 listed above. An unbeatable dollar value. The lowest price ever quoted for a complete Williamson Type Amplifier circuit. Model W-4M consists of main amplifier and power supply on single chassis. Shpg. Wt. 28 lbs., Express only ........................ **$39.75**
Model W-4 consists of W-4M plus WA-P2 Preamplifier. Shpg. Wt. 35 lbs., Express only ...... **$59.50**

homes of enthusiasts in search of good sound reproduction. Unless built into customized furniture, most such equipment made few concessions to domestic interiors. What's more, people often had to build the equipment themselves. The Williamson amplifier circuits – first published in the UK in 1947 – were widely followed; many companies sold parts or complete amplifiers based on them. Among these were Dynaco and Heathkit (see left), whose constructional kits were very popular in the '50s and '60s.

Even where chassis were bought ready-built, they often came without a case, and had to be installed at home in wall units or bookshelves. The power amplifier was usually mounted out of sight and connected to a separate unit with all the controls mounted for convenient access. These were comprehensive and included a range of equalizers (to match the recording characteristics of different record companies, which were not as yet standardized) as well as filters to mask scratches and motor noise from records. Control fascias were typically of brass or copper colour, while the chassis were often finely finished, even though not on view.

## US pioneers

Fisher and Scott were two names in the young US hi-fi industry of the '40s and '50s who went on to produce quality mainstream equipment. In 1946, Avery Fisher's company (see right) brought out one of the first true home hi-fi systems. The company founded in 1947 ►►

**FISHER 80C**

Avery Fisher's company – whose products proudly bore the legend "The Fisher" – helped to pioneer the "modular" approach to home hi-fi. Enthusiasts could start with one sound source – such as a radio – and then add others as their budget allowed, rather than having to buy everything at once and risking inferior quality. At this stage hi-fi units still bore many of the hallmarks of professional equipment, and the 80C control unit provided not only comprehensive equalization for records and tape but also studio-style mixing and fading for up to five channels. In 1956 the 80C cost $100. A wooden cabinet was extra, as buyers often mounted the equipment in a customized console.

◄

date of introduction: **1955, US**

size: **32 x 20 x 11cm (12³/₄ x 7³/₄ x 4¹/₄in)**

key features: **early hi-fi control unit; studio-style features**

◄ Before the LP came along an album really was an album: it was a set of 78rpm discs packaged together to look like a book.

## the LP and the coming of pop

In the early '50s pop didn't really exist. As 78s gave way to microgrooves, it was the well-off middle-aged who bought the first LPs – the Broadway cast recordings and Sinatra albums. Six big labels controlled the US record industry, and it was a similar story in the UK.

But change was coming: in the US the number of independent radio stations tripled between 1946 and 1956, many playing blues, gospel, or country. Others were launching the news and top forty formats we still have today. Independent labels too – Chess in Chicago, Atlantic in New York, Sam Phillips's Sun in Memphis – were building bridges between black blues and rhythm & blues and between white pop and country.

By the early '50s this fusion had been dubbed "rock'n'roll" by Alan Freed, a DJ working at station WJW Cleveland. Then, in 1955, Elvis Presley was signed from Sun to RCA for a then astonishing $35,000, and was lobbed like a hand grenade into the heart of mainstream American culture, predictably outraging it in the process. But in "Heartbreak Hotel" and "Blue Suede Shoes", teenagers sensed a new era – even in the UK, where the BBC played little American pop. For the first time young people had money to spend on records by singers little older than they were.

Rock'n'roll was too limited a style for continued record sales and radio airplay, but Tin Pan Alley's songwriters captured teenage pleasures and pains in two minutes of catchy pop that still had a strong rock beat. Records were cut at higher sound levels, with the singer closely miked for maximum impact. The singer needed to be young and attractive, but music-wise the real power had begun to shift to the producer.

◄ As well as developing the first solid-body electric guitar, Les Paul had hits with Mary Ford in the early '50s using multi-track recording and overdubbing techniques that were years ahead of their time.

▼ Decca may have missed out on the Beatles ten years later, but the company was technologically ahead of EMI in the '50s. This 1952 advertisement mocked EMI's thirty-four 78s of Wagner's *Die Meistersinger*, comparing them with Decca's infinitely more portable six LPs.

six *versus* thirty-four!

## SCOTT 310C

In 1954 the US hi-fi company Scott produced a one-box amplifier with the tubes mounted horizontally, allowing a compact horizontal style for component hi-fi that has lasted ever since. The 310 series of "broadcast monitors" began in the same year. It was the first wide-band FM tuner with exceptional sound quality, free from noise and tuning drift. Later versions added a precision vernier tuning dial (on the right) typical of many Scott tuners of the era, while the illuminated meter measured signal strength. *High Fidelity* magazine said it was "as close to perfection as is possible at this time".

▼

date of introduction: **1954-62, US**

size: **13 x 38 x 33cm (5 x 15 x 13 in)**

key features: **wide-band FM coverage; precision tuning**

by H.H.Scott introduced in 1954 a one-box hi-fi amplifier which had tubes that were mounted horizontally instead of vertically. It achieved a compact horizontal style for hi-fi separates which has persisted ever since.

The high quality of Marantz and McIntosh equipment from the '50s and '60s is still admired and sought after by audiophiles today. Working with audio engineers Sidney Smith and Dick Sequerra, Saul Marantz built a series of tube hi-fi components (see right) that became yardsticks for the hi-fi industry. By 1949 Frank H.McIntosh had designed a low distortion fifty-watt amplifier, and this was followed by a series of others in the '50s and '60s, constructed on gleaming chrome chassis (see p.56).

Meanwhile the company named after its founders Sidney Harman and Bernard Kardon was among the first with an AM/FM stereo receiver (see right), and was also renowned for the Citation series of hi-fi components in the late '50s and '60s.

### The start of British hi-fi

From the late '40s H.J.Leak was at the forefront of the British hi-fi industry. Like many of his US counterparts, Leak had an early career installing amplifiers in theatres and cinemas. In 1945 he announced the Point One series of amplifiers (see p.28), whose name derives from its distortion levels of less than 0.1 per cent. Post-war shortages meant the UK market was slow to take off, but Leak toured Britain in the '50s, spreading the word with hi-fi demonstrations. ►►

## HARMAN KARDON
## FESTIVAL RECEIVER

Harman Kardon was among the first
to market an integrated AM/FM
stereo receiver in a style that looks
familiar today. It featured a thirty-watt
power amplifier, control unit, and
completely separate AM and FM
tuners and front-panel scales –
simulcast AM and FM transmissions
were still seen as a possible way of
transmitting the left and right stereo
channels. With its "dramatic new"
copper fascia and walnut or
fruitwood case, it cost $300.

## MARANTZ MODEL 7
## PRE-AMPLIFIER

Working with the engineers Sidney
Smith and Dick Sequerra, Saul
Marantz (1902–97) built tube hi-fi
components that soon became
benchmarks for the industry. The
model 7 was a stereo pre-amplifier
for use with either the model 8B
power amplifier or two massive
seventy-watt model 9 mono
amplifiers. Despite its wide range of
equalization, monitoring, and filters,
the careful, ergonomic design makes
it look uncluttered. Costing $264
at launch, the model 7 sold over
100,000 units and was reintroduced
in a classic edition in the mid 1990s.

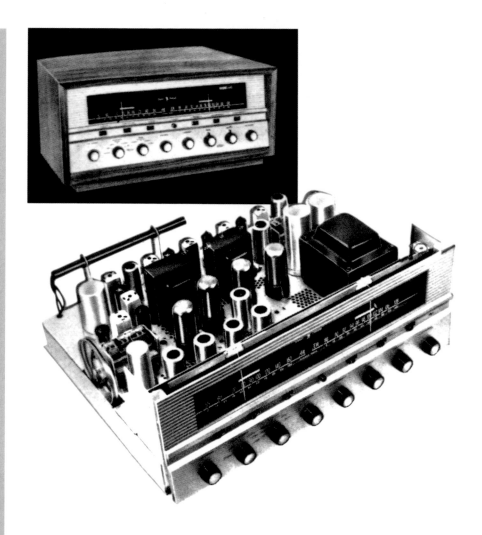

▲

date of introduction: **1959, US**

size: **40 x 15 x 33 cm (15¾ x 6 x 13 in)**

key features: **early receiver; stereo-
ready**

▼

date of introduction: **1959, US**

size: **38 x 15 x 23 cm (15 x 6 x 9 in)**

key features: **comprehensive controls
and inputs; high-quality construction**

## QUAD QCII CONTROL UNIT

The QCII was a mono control unit designed for use with the Quad II power amplifier launched the same year. Tone, filtering, and equalization adjustments were comprehensive, but edge-controlled knobs and push buttons kept the front panel uncluttered, while Quad's classically understated "silver fawn" and brown styling harmonized with home interiors of the period. The QCII ran until 1967, though the Quad 22 stereo version (see p.55) became the more popular choice after its launch in 1959.

▼

date of introduction: **1953, UK**

size: **26.5 x 9 x 16.5 cm (10¹/₂ x 3¹/₂ x 6¹/₂ in)**

key features: **comprehensive filters; distinctive ergonomics**

The famous Quad company founded by Peter Walker also had its origins in public-address equipment before crossing over into home audio. The company's power amplifier and control unit (see left), as well as the first ever full-range electrostatic loudspeaker (see p.39), were enduring products from the 50s. Another British company, Lowther, had produced top-quality radio and amplifier chassis since the 1930s. These had usually been teamed with horn loudspeakers (see p.38) designed by the pioneering Paul Voigt company. From the late '40s, Voigt speaker production continued under Lowther's name and control, and a series of pioneering drive units and cabinet designs followed. Other key names of the era were Wharfedale and Goodmans, which specialized in drive units for enthusiasts who wanted to build their own cabinets. The founder of Wharfedale, Gilbert Briggs, published an influential series of books on speakers, and joined Quad's Peter Walker to give sell-out demonstrations of live versus recorded sound in London and New York which showed what huge advances had been made.

### Turning the tables

Automatic changers that stacked a pile of ten records were popular in the early days, especially in the US. British maker Garrard had made record changers since the 1930s and by the '50s refined three-speed versions of these were very successful. But with the coming of the LP, high-quality "transcription" turntables became more popular, for example Garrard's 301 and Thorens' TD124 (see right). These sacrificed convenience in favour of precision engineering, and had a high-quality tone-arm mounted alongside. Such equipment still sounds good today and has a devoted following of collectors and restorers.

The arm might be fitted with a cartridge from early pioneers like Denon of Japan, or Ortofon of Denmark. Both companies grew ▶▶

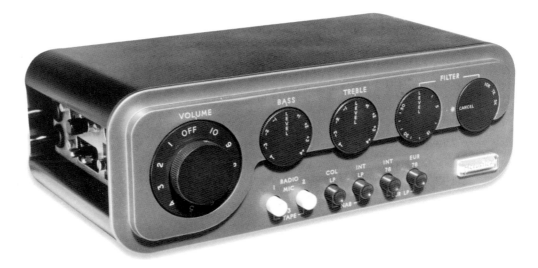

▶

date of introduction: **1953, UK**

size: **37x35cm (14½x13¾in)**

key features: **early home hi-fi turntable; idler drive; fine speed control**

## GARRARD 301

The 301 transcription turntable was designed for the BBC, but soon gained a wider reputation as a high-quality home hi-fi unit. The 401 of 1965 is similar but with sharper '60s styling. Both are now sought by collectors and restorers, and a new British company, Loricraft, has refined the design into the "501".

## THORENS TD124

On idler-drive turntables, motor vibrations could be heard as a low-pitched rumble. The TD124 used a combination belt/idler wheel drive to reduce this, and looked forward to the fully belt-driven turntables of later decades. A clutched two-piece platter allowed a quick start-up and the side panel simplified tone-arm mounting.

▼

date of introduction: **1958, Switzerland**

size: **39.5x32.5cm (15½x12¾in)**

key features: **idler/belt-drive, two-part platter, fine speed control**

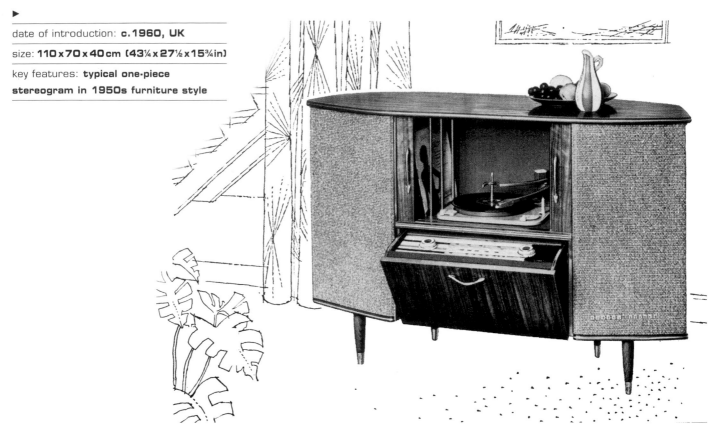

date of introduction: **c.1960, UK**

size: **110 x 70 x 40 cm (43¼ x 27⅛ x 15¾in)**

key features: **typical one-piece stereogram in 1950s furniture style**

## SOBELL STEREOGRAM

Sobell was a company that sold radiograms through furniture stores rather than audio equipment shops. On this typical British "stereogram" from the end of the 50s, the cocktail-cabinet styling includes a record-changer compartment hidden behind sliding doors, and a pull-down flap for the radio controls. The whole is supported on spindly legs. Such stereograms were always a poor compromise because, apart from other failings, the built-in speakers were too close together for satisfactory stereo separation. In any case, at this time stereo was available only from records, not from the radio.

from involvement with film sound and record-cutting equipment, and set lasting standards for moving-coil cartridge design in the 1950s.

## Hi-fi and the domestic interior

The growth of hi-fi sometimes created tension within the home, as the demands of a mainly male hobby and female views on domestic harmony conflicted. Hi-fi magazines were full of laboured humour about "pacifying the wife", while periodicals such as *Life* put the female perspective with despairing talk of husbands as "hi-fi addicts". Women were said to hate the "trailing wires" and clutter, and their husbands' tendency to play hi-fi at maximum volume. One answer to the clutter problem was to enclose equipment in a custom-made furniture-style cabinet, sold in period as well as contemporary designs. *Hi-Fi News* said that existing furniture could be adapted, advising "a lady's dressing-table is often suitable, fulfilling the technical requirements without being vulgar".

## Loudspeaker legends

Often loudspeakers meant an excursion into DIY, with enthusiasts fitting speaker "drive units" into a large wooden cabinet or vertical concrete pipe, for example. Some designers recommended the "draped" loudspeaker option: wall-hung speaker boxes concealed behind a thin floor-to-ceiling fabric saved money because they need not be furniture-finished ▶▶

## DOMESTIC INTERIORS

In the 1950s many enthusiasts had to find a way of integrating what looked like lab equipment into the domestic setting – especially difficult in period homes. The American magazine *High Fidelity* noted in 1955 that many readers had traditional furnishings, though the system shown below is of relatively modern design. In the UK, one-piece units for installing everything except the loudspeakers were available in Queen Anne or Sheraton styles, while the prestige London retailer Imhof boasted that "we have hidden speakers in chimneys, in ceilings, and in the minstrel gallery of a baronial hall". In contrast, the leading London modern furniture store Heals designed a contemporary custom cabinet to house Quad equipment (see p. 55).

## Record Housing

*are proud to present their new*

### MADRIGAL

#### Hi-Fi Equipment Cabinet

Built by craftsmen from solid materials, exquisitely finished in burr walnut, the dignified lines of the Madrigal will grace the most elegant of homes. Although moderate in size it has been intelligently designed to hold all the following equipment: 1. Turntable (transcription or auto-change) 2. Tape deck 3. Main amplifier 4. Pre-amplifier and radio tuner (behind left-hand door) 5. One hundred records.

Dimensions: 37" wide × 34" high (including 9" legs) × 18½" deep.

Price: 55 gns.

If you give us your nearest main shopping centres, we can advise you of your local Record Housing Stockist. Write to Dept HN/960

**RECORD HOUSING**

Brook Rd, London, N.22. BOWes Park 7487/8

▲ A typical British period-style hi-fi cabinet dating from 1960.

▼ This American furniture for housing audio equipment dates from the late '50s.

▲ ►

date of introduction: **1949, US**

designer: **Paul Klipsch**

size: **127 x 76 x 68 cm (50 x 30 x 26³/₄in)**

key feature: **innovative folded-horn design**

THE AUTHENTIC **Klipschorn**

FOR PERFECTIONISTS WHO CAN BOTH APPRECIATE AND AFFORD THE BEST SOUND REPRODUCTION

## KLIPSCHORN

In the 1950s horn speakers were often used as they were particularly efficient, but they had to be huge in order for the bass to register properly. Paul Klipsch in the US patented a system whereby the horn was "folded" into a complex labyrinth within the outer cabinet, reducing it to a size that was suitable for the average-sized home. The Klipschorn, launched in 1949, used the room corner to add to the horn's effect. The Klipschorn is still in production and a more recent version is also shown. Horn speakers rapidly went out of fashion with the advent of stereo, as few rooms had two suitable corners, but they are cult products again today.

and, in the early stereo days, were said to give a more convincing "sound stage" by preventing the eye from focusing on the speakers.

The speakers of the '40s had to be efficient at converting power into sound because the triode tubes then used in amplifiers gave limited output. Horn speakers gave high efficiency but, for good bass response, had to be enormous. Paul Klipsch's influential folded-horn design (see left) was rather more practical in normal-sized rooms. In the UK there were designs from Lowther and Tannoy (see right), while in the US models like the Electrovoice Patrician and James B. Lansing's Hartsfield and Paragon (see p.40) combined imposing size with superb craftsmanship.

In Britain Stanley Kelly's innovative high-frequency speaker unit used a vibrating aluminium ribbon instead of a cone, while Quad's full-range electrostatic loudspeaker broke new ground in performance and appearance by nearly doing away with a cabinet altogether (see right).

### The advent of stereo

By the end of the '50s recognizably modern "integrated" hi-fi components were becoming available. They were free-standing, needed no building in, and suited smaller homes. Loudspeakers could be smaller too, and here Edgar Villchur's Acoustic Research company (see p.59), led the way with the "acoustic suspension" principle, which gave much better bass reproduction than had been possible from a small cabinet. ▶▶

## TANNOY GRF CORNER HORN

Tannoy is a long-established British company whose corner horn designs became lasting classics. Founded as long ago as 1926 by Guy R. Fountain, Tannoy became synonymous with public-address loudspeakers. It pioneered "dual concentric" loudspeaker drive units (with a small, high-frequency horn built into the centre of a large bass cone), which enthusiasts could install in their own cabinets if they wished. This diagram of the GRF Corner Horn shows how sound from the rear of the speaker cone passes through a folded-horn arrangement before leaving the cabinet at the sides.

## QUAD ESL

In 1957, Quad broke new ground in performance and appearance by virtually abolishing the need for a cabinet. In this, the world's first full-range electrostatic loudspeaker, the sound came from three electrically charged plastic membranes stretched between perforated metal plates to which the amplifier output was connected. The lightness of the membranes and the absence of a boxy cabinet gave a more accurate, transparent, and uncoloured sound than most cone-type speakers. They also permitted the ESL's uniquely slim and easily movable "firescreen" shape (designed by Christopher Heal).

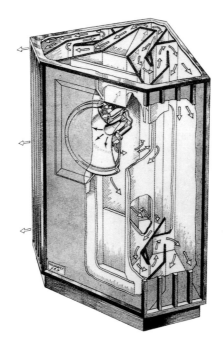

◄

date of introduction: **1955, UK**

size: **122 x 96.5 x 73.5 (48 x 38 x 29 in)**

key features: **corner horn; dual concentric drive units**

▶

date of introduction: **1957, UK**

size: **78.5 x 86 x 26.5 cm (31 x 34 x 10½ in)**

key features: **full-range electrostatic design; light, slim shape**

date of introduction: **1957, US**

designer: **Arnold Wolf**

size: **86.5 x 62 x 269cm**
**(34 x 24½ x 106in)**

key feature: **unique one-piece stereo**
**speaker system**

## JBL PARAGON

After the Hartsfield corner horn, James B. Lansing produced this unique design, made from 1957 to 1983. Originally designed as a central speaker between left and right to improve the stereo effect, the Paragon was revised to become a stand-alone stereo unit. Mid-range units at the side fire towards the curved wood panel, which reflects the sound into the room. The complex hand-built cabinet also had two treble and two bass units and cost from $1830.

## DECCA DECOLA

In the late 1940s the Decola record player had a state-of-the-art pick-up with sapphire stylus which did justice to Decca's "full frequency range recording" discs. This luxurious stereo Decola was fitted with Decca's unique stereo cartridge.

▼

date of introduction: **1960, UK**

size: **179 x 94 x 54.5cm**
**(70½ x 36½ x 21½ in)**

key features: **high-quality record player**
**with optional radio; fourteen speakers**

▶▶

date of introduction: **1960, US**

size: **16.5 x 24 x 33 cm (6½ x 9½ x 13 in)**

key features: **printed circuits; thirty-five**
**watts per channel**

Back in the 1930s key patents for stereo disc cutting and reproduction had been granted to the EMI engineer Alan Blumlein. Experiments with tape now showed how a convincing stereo effect could be recreated using two or more microphones, and two-channel recording and replay, through two loudspeakers. But much work had to be done to agree the means to combine two channels into one disc groove to be tracked by a single stylus.

Not many years after the LP's arrival, in 1957–8 stereo was launched. With demonstrations of ping-pong balls bouncing between left and right speakers, it seemed at first to be more about gimmickry than music. The demand for cheap stereo equipment led to some manufacturers cutting corners and pundits pronouncing that mediocre stereo was worse than good mono. But techniques improved, acceptance grew, and record companies began rebuilding their catalogues in stereo. Stereo radio broadcasts also started, using simultaneous transmissions on AM and FM frequencies, or FM and TV sound, for the two channels.

Most of the major brands had stereo equipment in their ranges by 1959. Few rooms could accommodate two large speaker cabinets, and this hastened the adoption of smaller systems. Stereo was soon seen as a status symbol, and this helped to bring hi-fi to wider attention, though the popular press still saw it as a slightly eccentric hobby.

## DYNACO STEREO 70

Founded in 1955 by David Hafler and Ed Laurent, Dynaco became a big name in high value hi-fi kits in the 1950s. They patented the 'ultralinear' circuit using special output transformers to give power with low distortion. As stereo came onstream at the end of the decade, Dynaco introduced their Stereo 70 kit which became one of the most popular tubed power amplifiers ever built, with over half a million sold. With the step by step instructions supplied it could be assembled in around 5 hours. The model shown is the authentic 1992 revival. Hafler himself became known for early patents in surround-sound technique.

▲ High kitsch today, perhaps, but, as the '60s were dawning, exotic shapes and finishes were just a way of adding appeal for young consumers.

# 1960-1969 **stereo** takes off

The 1960s were the age of the transistor, but they also saw the start of the hi-fi boom and the launch of the cassette.

## The transistor age

At the start of the 1960s the transistor radio market was booming, but manufacturers in Europe and the US were finding it ever harder to compete with Japanese imports. For a time they managed to compete on larger radios and record players, but in a few years these also would mostly be imported, even if they sometimes continued to carry the badge of a US or European company.

Far Eastern manufacturers specialized in pocket transistor sets. Most of these came with a single earpiece for private listening, but the quality in those days was little better than the sound from a telephone. However, having shown what could be done to miniaturize technology, tiny sets tended to fade away as the '60s progressed; buyers preferred equipment that would give rather more bass.

The start of the decade saw radios shifting away from the bright plastics of the late 1950s. Now the look was more often black or wood-grain-effect plastic, or real or fake leather; while trims, previously brass or gilt, were now usually chrome or satin aluminium. This combination became a universal aesthetic, often sourced in the Far East and sold worldwide. One short-lived idiom was a heavy-duty "combat" look, which lent many cheap portable radios an aura of military toughness and efficiency. ▶▶

### AMERICANA FP80

By the end of the 1950s the American radio industry was finding it impossible to compete with cheap imports from Japan. As well as now-familiar names like Sony (see p.14) and Hitachi, the market was flooded with cheap pocket sets with various American-sounding brand names, which were sold through drugstores or mail-order catalogues rather than through radio stores. The Americana FP80 was just one of thousands of such sets. The gilt trim, thumb-wheel controls, and much-vaunted number of transistors are typical of the genre. British makers, too, found they could not beat low-cost imports, and the Perdio (see opposite) was made for them in Hong Kong.

▶

date of introduction: **1962, Japan**

size: **10 x 7 x 3 cm (4 x 2¾ x 1¼ in)**

key features: **US-sounding brand; number of transistors promoted**

▶ The "bandspread" setting on this 1964 Perdio was supposed to aid tuning to the pop stations Radio Luxembourg and Radio Caroline.

## SINCLAIR MICRO 6

Clive Sinclair would become famous for a number of high-tech products at very low prices including calculators, digital watches, and the ZX80 and Spectrum home computers. However, among Sinclair's first ventures were tiny personal radio kits. Radio-building was still popular with hobbyists, fascinated by miniature equipment (in the days before microchips made it easier to achieve). The Micro 6 kit cost 59s 6d (just under £3), and was widely advertised in the British hobby press. The transistors used were allegedly rejects from early computer manufacturing and getting the set to work once built could be difficult. Sinclair "hi-fi" amplifiers followed later in the decade.

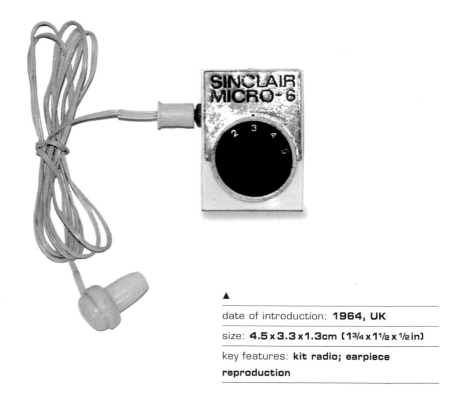

▲

date of introduction: **1964, UK**

size: **4.5 x 3.3 x 1.3cm (1³/₄ x 1¹/₂ x ¹/₂ in)**

key features: **kit radio; earpiece reproduction**

## "RADIO" RADIO

As the miniaturization and mass production that the transistor had helped bring about collided with an exuberant pop culture, radios became cheap, disposable commodities, their shape and structure no longer dictated by their function or the size of internal components. Fun radios lurked in Coca-Cola cans or cuddly toys. This radio proclaimed its "radio-ness" not by its functional form but by becoming a typographical device in its own right. Its provenance is uncertain, though it often features in collections of '60s design.

Such stylings might be condemned by the pundits of "good design", but in the heady climate of the new decade the symbolic role of products in people's lives was being taken more seriously. As Reyner Banham, a perceptive critic of design and popular culture, noted in 1963, "Pop design exists to be seen by other people... the mere possession of a far-out transistor set adds inches to the height, just as a loaded gun does in a Western." In any case, global mass production was beginning to marginalize well-meaning attempts by design élites to steer public taste.

### European styles

There were, however, distinctive styles outside the mass market. By the end of the '50s the Italian economy was growing rapidly and developing a strong export market for consumer goods. For the most part these were not technologically innovative; what they did have, however, was a visual symbolism that to an increasingly design-conscious world represented high style and fashionable living. Italian cars, scooters, furniture, lighting, TVs, and other products became the essence of chic to consumers worldwide. Neo-modernist designs in bright primary colours, like Brionvega's cube radio of 1964 (see opposite), had a strong appeal for well-off young consumers and helped to give plastic a new image of upmarket elegance.

In Germany Braun produced radios and hi-fi systems with a stripped-down aesthetic that was even more unornamented and functional than it had been in the '50s, and in 1961 Dieter Rams was appointed head ▶▶

## BRIONVEGA TS502

Brionvega was one of several Italian companies investing in design innovation in the '60s, raising the international status of Italian products as chic and desirable possessions, and producing a number of design classics. The TS502 is a neat high-tech design in two hinged sections. Shown half-open here, the two halves when fully open lock together with a magnet. Fully closed, they form a neat box concealing the controls and speaker. Sapper (b.1932) and Zanuso (1916-2001) also collaborated on stylish "black cube" portable televisions for Brionvega.

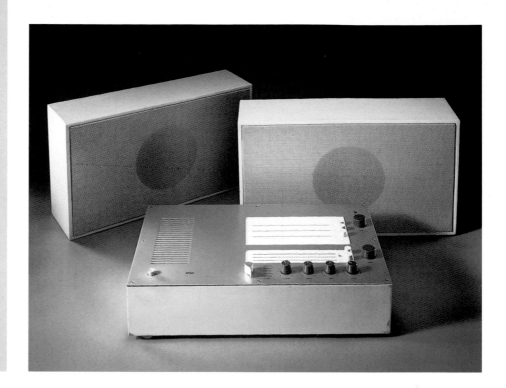

▼

date of introduction: **1964, Italy**

designer: **Marco Zanuso and Richard Sapper**

size: **22 x 13 x 13 cm (8³/₄ x 5 x 5 in)**

key features: **AM/FM transistor; portable either open or closed**

▲ The Braun TS45 Steuergerät stereo system (1965) was designed by Dieter Rams.

◄ US music producer Phil Spector used small speakers as well as studio monitors to make sure his unique "wall sound" still sounded good on a cheap radio. At first he refused to make stereo records, reputedly wearing a badge saying "Back to Mono".

# from pop to progressive

By the early '60s pop was a well-established commodity. This was a time of belief in limitless technological progress; products were new and exciting, affordable and expendable. In the UK, a transistor radio was used to listen to Radio Luxembourg or the offshore pirate stations, offering a glamorously rebellious alternative to the staid BBC.

Nineteen sixty-four saw the highest-ever sales of singles, while EP (Extended Play) discs were a popular four-song package with at least a couple of previous hits and a picture sleeve, which outsold LPs in the early years of the decade. The early to mid '60s were the perfect pop moment, with not only the Beatles and the Stones but labels such as Tamla Motown, '60s soul from Stax and Atlantic, and R&B-based groups such as the Who, the Kinks, which headed the "British Invasion" of the US. Phil Spector's "wall of sound" epitomized the rise of the producer over the artist.

From the late '60s pop began to fragment. *Sergeant Pepper* made pop music a respectable art form, and shifted fans' attention from live to recorded product. The record industry discovered targeted marketing, and "progressive" rock concept albums came out on niche labels to distinguish them from pop, while the sonic complexity of these albums chimed with the higher-grade stereo equipment coming on to the mass market.

Rock's increasing sophistication in the late '60s spurred the development of multi-track recording. The Beatles, under their producer George Martin, experimented with tape loops, over-dubs, and other effects. For prog rock, multi-tracking offered new possibilities for building a multi-layered orchestral sound.

▲ George Martin encouraged the Beatles' experiments with studio technique and classical arrangements. His pioneering multi-tracking on *Sergeant Pepper's Lonely Hearts Club Band* (1967), which used just three four-track tape machines synchronized together, changed the landscape of music production.

◄ Producer Joe Meek created innovative low-budget effects with compression, over-dubbing, backward tape playing, and echoing spaces such as stairwells. For the Tornados' 1962 hit "Telstar" he created synthesized pop twenty years ahead of its time.

## PYE 1207 STEREOGRAM

In the '50s Geoffrey Imhof, head of an upmarket London audio store, had told the Pye company that it needed products in a modern idiom in its range, and introduced it to the young furniture designer Robin Day (b.1915). This was the start of a long relationship with Pye, though Day's TV and radio cabinets, with their squared edges and matt finishes, were at odds with the curved, high-gloss, gilt-trimmed cabinets generally thought saleable in '50s Britain. By the '60s contemporary tastes in furniture were catching up with the understated low-line teak cabinet of his 1207 radiogram.

▶

date of introduction: **1964, UK**

designer: **Robin Day**

size: **140 x 60 x 50cm (55 x 24 x 20 in)**

key features: **teak cabinet; vinyl front; modern appearance**

of design. In Denmark Bang & Olufsen, in the hands of its chief designer, Jakob Jensen, was, by the end of the '60s, refining a modern, slimmer, and sleeker look for its radios, record players, and tuner amplifiers. This would help the company carve out a successful niche market in the next decade.

Not all companies relied upon the flair of individuals in this way. In the '50s and '60s Philips grew into an international company based in Eindhoven in the Netherlands. Like many large organizations, it was at first resistant to change, and new ideas from designers were often thwarted by interdepartmental tensions. But, under the supervision of the former architect Rein Veersema, Philips introduced its Design Bureau with a systematic strategy covering every aspect of the design process across the company. By the late '60s Philips had developed a stronger corporate identity across its many divisions and "families" of products (such as radios and cassette players) with a clearly recognizable Philips style had been introduced. This strategy helped the company compete relatively successfully with Japan in the mass market during the coming decades.

### Music on the move

Radios had been fitted to some luxury cars ever since the 1930s, but there were significant problems, including interference from the car's electrical system and high noise levels inside the vehicle. Another difficulty was the fact that, in order to work effectively, valves required a much higher voltage than a car battery could provide. Typically, a car radio ▶▶

▶

date of introduction: **1960s, UK**

key features: **mass appeal, low price**

▼

date of introduction: **1960s, US**

key feature: **integrated design**

## DANSETTE

Record players from British maker Dansette were cheap, simple and popular with teenagers, though this early 1960s brochure features the slightly more upmarket "Hi-Fi" model which claimed to be "designed to meet the exacting requirements of the connoisseur".

## CADILLAC CAR RADIO

The radio of a 1964 Cadillac DeVille. In the late '50s, smaller components led to integrated car radios which could be built into the dashboard. In the '60s came all-transistor models, often with push-button controls and a cartridge or cassette player.

chassis would come in two parts: a high-voltage converter and amplifier mounted near the floor or in the engine compartment, with the tuner and controls on the dashboard or the steering column. In the late '50s new valves and the first transistors were combined to produce a much more compact one-piece car radio. These were followed in the late '60s by all-transistor models, often with push-button station selection (a big advantage for the driver) and a cartridge or cassette player. Standardization of the size of the slot required for mounting a car radio later helped to create a strong "aftermarket", as car owners wanted to install a radio, or upgrade to a better one.

## The record player grows up

Rock'n'roll and pop had already fuelled the market for 45rpm singles and portable record players, and demand rocketed with the rise of the Beatles and other British and American groups in the early '60s (see pp.48–9). The British company Dansette, for example, produced huge numbers of portable record players (see p.51), with a "swinging '60s" aura that is irresistible to collectors today.

Smaller, battery-powered record players came in plastic cabinets with the speaker mounted in the lid (see right). Though sound quality was poor and the volume limited by today's standards, they were portable and stylish and, most importantly, affordable. As sales of long-playing albums grew during the '60s, multi-disc record-changers went into a decline. ▶▶

### TEPPAZ BI-BALAD

This small record player from France had its loudspeaker mounted in the detachable lid. The transistorized circuit could be operated from batteries or from mains current. The fabric-covered fibreboard case in the style of light hand luggage conveys a strong message of portability. Teppaz claimed in the accompanying text to offer "12 models in 18 colours" – such a profusion of choice being very much a part of the new consumer culture. The model name is interesting, "balade" being French for a stroll or saunter. In the 1980s "baladeur" would be adopted as the French word for a Walkman.

▶

date of introduction: **1960s, France**

size: **37 x 23 x 15 cm (14⅛ x 9 x 6 in)**

key features: **solid-state amplifier; battery or mains operation**

## PHILIPS GF303

Circles and spheres were key elements of much '60s pop design, and this is a neat example with the lid, tone-arm, loudspeaker capsule, and recessed volume control all echoing the circular structure, which is itself exactly the diameter of an LP record. The transparent polystyrene lid came in red or blue.

▶

date of introduction: **1969, Netherlands**

designer: **Patrice Dupont**

size: **30 cm dia x 12 cm high (12 x 4¾ in)**

key features: **portable player with '60s styling; lid-mounted speaker**

▲ This "unit audio" from British maker Ferguson marked the beginning of a shift from one-piece radiograms to separates.

▶

date of introduction: **1965, Italy**

designer: **Achille Castiglioni**

size: **75 x 123 x 36 cm (29½ x 48½ x 14¼in)**

key features: **movable, adaptable speaker arrangement**

## BRIONVEGA RR126

Achille (b.1918) was the youngest of the three Castiglioni brothers, who were a powerful force in modern Italian design. Here he frees the radio-gramophone from its static image by mounting it on a steel frame with castors. The loudspeakers can be lifted off (note the recessed handles) and hooked on to the sides of the centre unit, or stored on top to create a neat box structure. The main unit contains an AM/FM radio and amplifier, and on top an automatic record deck with its own clear acrylic lid. To balance the high-tech shape and clinical laminated surfaces, there is a humanizing touch in the face-like arrangement of dials and controls on the front.

As stereo caught on, the one-piece "stereogram" became fashionable (see p.50). But the distance between the left and right loudspeakers was too small for proper stereo and it was only a matter of time before these were split off as separate units (see p.53). In fact, as the '60s progressed, increasing affluence made the whole idea of hi-fi equipment more desirable, while the higher production values of progressive rock albums also called for something better than a cheap portable player.

This made two things happen: designers of genuine hi-fi gave more thought to its appearance, while at the same time mainstream companies revamped their radiograms and record players to give a more technical "separates" look, which was often called "unit audio" or similar. This was not just a marketing trick: separates were genuinely better suited to the shelving units, room dividers, and other flexible informal furniture finding its way into modern homes.

Audio equipment was also following the trend towards lighter, Scandinavian styling in furniture. Gradually during the '60s matt teak veneers, aluminium panels, and uncluttered, rectangular shapes began to replace the darker, shinier finishes of the '50s.

The move away from furniture style radiograms to an "instrument" look for audio was in some ways what "good design" propagandists had argued for earlier. But in truth, rather than fulfilling a design ideal, the look was just another style in an increasingly crowded marketplace. Compared to Braun's for example, most of the new equipment was anything but unornamented – the "ornament" was merely in a technical idiom. ▶▶

date of introduction: **1959, UK**

size: **26.5 x 9 x 15 cm (10½ x 3½ x 6 in)**

key features: **comprehensive filters; distinctive ergonomic design**

▼

date of introduction: **1968, Italy**

designer: **Mario Bellini**

size: **21.5 x 20 x 8 cm (8½ x 8¾ x 3¼ in)**

key features: **slot-in 45 rpm player; retractable handle**

## QUAD 22

This typical early '60s hi-fi furniture is fitted with a Quad 22 stereo control unit and Quad FM tuner. As stereo caught on, the 22 rather than the mono QCII (see p.34) would be used with a pair of Quad II power amplifiers installed out of sight, though Quad's elegant ergonomic design was little changed. The 22 ran until 1967, when it was replaced by the transistorized model 33.

## MINERVA GA45 POP

Mario Bellini (b.1935) was a key figure in the rising reputation of Italian design, and in 1963 he became chief design consultant for Olivetti. This plastic portable player, which he designed for Minerva, was also made under licence for Grundig, of which this is an example. The rounded shapes of Bellini's work in the '50s and '60s became more angular in the '70s (see p.89).

## McINTOSH MC275

McIntosh was another prestige American hi-fi maker in the same league as Marantz. The company was committed to careful engineering and conservatively rated components, and in an advertisement it claimed of its products that "like the classics, they endure". This was clearly true, as the MC275 was produced from 1961 to 1973, and then reintroduced in a limited edition (of which this is an example) in the 1990s to commemorate the late president of McIntosh, Gordon Gow. Elegantly fitted out in black and chrome, the MC275 had two powerful seventy-five-watt amplifiers on one chassis, and cost $444 in 1962. A comprehensively equipped range of McIntosh control units and tuners completed the picture.

Sony was a catalyst for this redefinition of the technological aesthetic: although the company's key product developments in the '60s were in television rather than audio, the Sony Design Centre (founded in Tokyo in 1961) became a model for the strategic use of design and marketing. It continually developed innovative high-tech products and at the same time expanded into new markets by freshening existing ones.

Meanwhile industry regroupings in Europe had left some companies with a portfolio of brands, which they took advantage of to sell to different market sectors using superficial styling differences. For example, in Britain, identical stereos were sold with a high-style black-and-white paint finish under the Ultra brand, and in teak under the more staid Ferguson and His Master's Voice names.

### Hi-fi goes solid state

The stereo boom at the start of the '60s saw US makers like Fisher and Scott slugging it out in the middle market – where the number of tubes and front-panel features was becoming more important than sound quality. On the other hand, respected brands like McIntosh and Marantz produced some of their finest products in the '60s (see left). Meanwhile FM radio took a big step forward in 1961 with the adoption of the Zenith/General Electric system for encoding stereo sound, which is still in use today. Broadcasting in stereo began that year in the US, though UK listeners had to wait until 1966 for BBC stereo. ▶▶

◀

date of introduction: **1961, US**

size: **43 x 30.5 x 20 cm (17 x 12 x 8 in)**

key features: **seventy-five watt per channel amplifier; high-quality finish**

▼ A mid '60s stereo receiver from Japanese maker Kenwood (branded Trio in the UK). Combined tuner/amplifiers were in fact more popular in the US, where there was a wider choice of radio stations.

date of introduction: **1970, US**

designer: **Arnold Wolf**

size: **36 x 60 x 35cm**
**(14¼ x 23½ x 13½ in)**

key features: **bass reflex design;
innovative grille**

## JBL L100 "CENTURY"

Though appearing at the start of the
'70s, the L100 was essentially a
simplified version of a successful
1960s James B. Lansing studio
monitor. Wanting to expand into the
consumer hi-fi market, JBL felt the
design's professional cachet would be
an added draw. Producing a
distinctive bookshelf loudspeaker is a
challenge for a designer because little
of it is visible except the front fabric.
After various experiments, Arnold
Wolf chose a plastic foam, which he
moulded with a waffle pattern to give
depth and interest to the front and
then sprayed it with a paint that
would not affect the acoustic
transparency. The successful
outcome represents one of the first
uses of strong colour in hi-fi styling.

At first the transistors used in radios and cheap equipment had neither
the power nor the bandwidth for serious hi-fi, but this was about to
change. Within a year or two valve/transistor "hybrids" and then
exclusively solid-state amplifiers and tuners began to appear. Cool-running
and up-to-the-minute, they swept valves away within a few years: this was
an age which did not question technical advances or have any love for old
technology for its own sake. Some critical listeners grumbled about the
"transistor sound", though by the end of the decade improved circuit
technique had converted most audiophiles to the solid-state cause. But
the warm, involving sound, plus the sheer physical presence and beauty of
much tubed equipment, would see a revival of interest from the late '70s.

Among the first British makers to produce transistorized hi-fi equipment
were Radford, and Leak with its Stereo 30 amplifier (see right) in 1963.
By 1967 Quad had entered the solid-state age with its long-running 303
power amplifier and 33 control unit. But the compactness of solid-state
designs led many makers to follow Leak and switch to integrated amplifiers.

By the mid '60s UK and US hi-fi companies were facing serious competition from imports, just as radio makers had earlier. At first through
small import companies, amplifiers, tuners, and receivers from then
unfamiliar names such as Hitachi, Pioneer, and Sansui began to appear in
shops. By the end of the decade many of the West's hi-fi manufacturers
were in retreat, and standards of design and manufacture often suffered
as they tried, mostly in vain, to compete in the mass market. There was ▶▶

## AR2AX LOUDSPEAKER

Acoustic Research pioneered smaller speakers using the "acoustic suspension" principle: a flexibly-mounted speaker cone sprung by the air inside the cabinet. The AR2ax (shown) was a smaller version of the earlier AR1. Henry Kloss, who worked for AR, was later a partner in speaker maker KLH.

## LEAK 30 AMPLIFIER

The Stereo 30 was one of the first British transistor hi-fi amplifiers. Leak claimed sound quality was as good as valves, but early solid-state models were not always praised. The Goodmans Maxim (also shown) was part of a trend for small book-shelf speakers.

▲

date of introduction: **1965, US**

size: **34.5 x 61 x 29 cm (13½ x 24 x 11½ in)**

key features: **small size; acoustic suspension design**

◄

date of introduction: **1963, UK**

size: **33 x 25.5 x 12.5 cm (13 x 10 x 5 in)**

key features: **early transistor stereo amplifier**

▶

date of introduction: **1966, Japan**

size: **72 x 60 cm dia (28 x 24 in)**

key features: **1960s pop styling; integrated tape player**

## WELTRON 2007

Circular and spherical designs on pedestals were the height of modernity in the '60s, the shape possibly reflecting a preoccupation with the aesthetics of space travel. Inside the "pod" is an automatic changer of the kind then fitted to most popular record players, plus controls for the AM/FM radio. At the front is the tape player: at first this was an eight-track cartridge unit (see p.66) but later this was replaced by the more popular cassette system.

Speaker design was still an art as much as a science, but new materials for drive-unit magnets and cone surrounds meant a small box could now give good bass reproduction. In the UK, Leak's Sandwich speaker was an innovative design: the bass speaker cone used a layer of expanded polystyrene sandwiched between layers of aluminium foil to give a lightweight but rigid, non-resonant structure.

In fact, speakers were one sector where the UK remained successful in the '60s and '70s. Tens of thousands of people buying their first "proper" hi-fi system opted for moderately sized and priced models like the Denton and Linton from Wharfedale, or one from the Celestion Ditton range. Goodmans led the trend towards compact bookshelf systems with its small Maxim speaker (see p.59) and the same sized Maxamp amplifier.

## Turntable trends

Good-quality, traditionally engineered turntables like Garrard's 401 (1965) and the Thorens models are typical of the '60s. But in 1961 Acoustic Research produced a ground-breaking belt-driven turntable with a sub-chassis suspended on springs (see p.62). Meanwhile the small British company SME was setting new standards for a precision-engineered universal pick-up arm. This was often partnered with cartridges from the US brand Shure, which had an unequalled reputation for tracking records without distortion at very low forces, so reducing record wear.

These were products for the well-off, however, and the integrated record deck, such as the budget-priced Garrard SP25 (see p.63), or the Swiss-made Goldring GL75 ready-mounted on a wooden plinth, was the norm for mass-market hi-fi enthusiasts.

## The cassette and cartridge arrive

In 1963 Philips used the Berlin Radio Show to launch a totally new format, and succeeded where other makers who had set out to offer the public foolproof tape-recording had failed. While it never reached the quality standards of vinyl or CD, the compact cassette would sell in huge numbers. Using tape only 2.5mm (1/8in) wide – half the width of the ▶▶

### THORENS TD150

With its TD150 turntable, Thorens maintained its tradition of high-quality engineering but followed the lead set by AR in the US (see p.62) in using a belt-drive and a sub-chassis suspended on springs that carried the platter and tone-arm and isolated them from vibration. But while the AR turntable came with its own tone-arm which could not easily be changed, the TD150 made it easy to fit tone-arms from different manufacturers (like the SME shown on p.63, for example). The majority of audiophile turntables designed since then have followed this basic design.

▶

date of introduction: **1965, Switzerland**

size: **39.5 x 32.5 cm (15½ x 12¾ in)**

key features: **belt-drive; suspended sub-chassis**

open-reel tape then in use on home recorders – and a slow tape speed, an hour or more of recording time could be fitted on to a convenient pocket-sized cassette. After starting out with recorders the size and shape of a shoebox, most makers had, by the end of the '60s, adopted the enduring concept of the combined portable radio-cassette.

But early cassette equipment left a lot to be desired: tape hiss, limited treble response, and unstable tape speed were all problems. Though tapes and recorders gradually improved over the years, really good sound from cassettes had to wait until the turn of the decade and a development by a company that would become a household name – Dolby.

The cassette wasn't the only packaged tape format. In the US there was a big demand for tapes that could be played on the road. In the early '60s, Ernie Muntz adapted an endless-loop tape cartridge originally developed for in-store displays and radio jingles, and marketed four-track players and pre-recorded tapes quite successfully. Then in 1965 William Powell Lear announced a refined eight-track version of the Muntz cartridge, backed by Ford (which fitted eight-track players in its new ranges) and by record company RCA Victor. At first the system sold mainly as an auto accessory, but, within a year or so, portable players and home systems incorporating eight-track were available. The eight-track system had a push-button track change which was convenient while driving, but many albums suffered musically through having to be split into four equal (stereo) sections.

## PHILIPS EL3300

In 1963 Philips launched a totally new tape format at the Berlin Radio Show. The cassette system was freely licensed to other makers and succeeded where earlier "fiddle-free" tape systems failed, selling in huge numbers over following decades. Most early cassette recorders were shoebox-shaped portables like this one and, as the supplied microphone suggests, were really only fit for voice recording. Though the quality of recorders and tapes gradually improved, really good sound from cassettes had to wait for Dolby's noise reduction system.

▶

date of introduction: **1963, Netherlands**

size: **20 x 11 x 5.5 cm (7¾ x 4¼ x 2¼in)**

key features: **battery operation; compact and easy-to-use tape format**

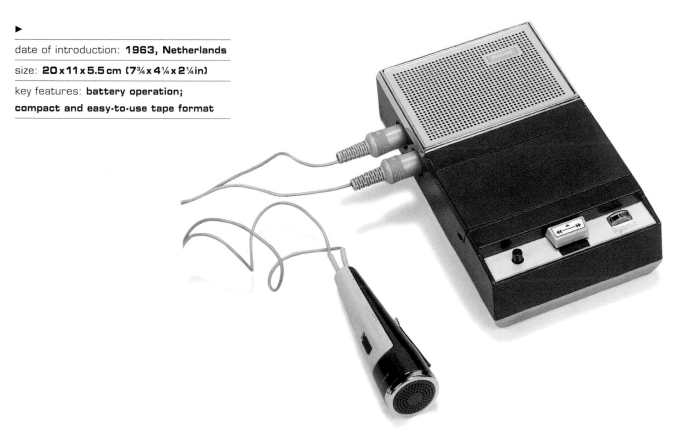

# If music be the food of love, it pays to have a Loudmouth.

GENERAL ELECTRIC

8 TRACK PROGRAM
**POWER SOUND**

## THE LOUDMOUTH
### PORTABLE 8-TRACK PLAYER

For tender moments, speak softly, but carry a Loudmouth. General Electric engineered this power sound 8-track cartridge player to give you a nifty combination of big sound with super mobility. You get a two-speaker system, a sing-along/PA mike, an optional car/boat adapter.

There's also automatic channel advance and tone control. Treble Red, Bass Blue or Gunmetal Gray. With adjustable shoulder/carry strap. And if you want big sound, super mobility, plus an FM/AM radio, ask to see GE's SHOWOFF.

## GENERAL **GE** ELECTRIC

Audio Electronics Products Department, Syracuse, N.Y. 13201

---

◄

date of introduction: **1960s, US**

key features: **portable 8-track player; "sing-along" microphone**

▼

date of introduction: **1960s, Netherlands**

key features: **cassette system; spherical shape**

### GE LOUDMOUTH 8-TRACK

Though the eight-track cartridge was first developed for car use, home systems and portable players like this one were soon available. But the smaller size and recording ability of cassettes saw them triumph by the '70s.

### PHILIPS VISION 2000

Another typically 1960s piece of futuristic design like the Weltron (see p.64). This rare Philips model, with its plastic body, chromed pedestal stand and tinted acrylic lid incorporates a cassette deck and push-button tuner/amplifier.

▲  The Panasonic Toot-a-Loop bangle
radio (1970) came in several bright
colours. It is now a collectable novelty.

# 1970-1979 **decks**&disco

The 1970s saw mass-market interest in hi-fi at its peak – and the start of an audiophile backlash favouring older technology.

## Japan takes over

By the start of the decade the consumer electronics industry had moved into stereo sound in a big way. Despite economic uncertainty and soaring oil prices, audio separates were healthy mainstream sellers and monthly hi-fi magazines grew fat with advertisements. By the start of the '70s, Japanese manufacturers had gained a large share of the audio equipment market in the US and Europe. Their designers had learned how to offer much of the precision and style of high-status European products, such as Nagra tape recorders and Leica cameras, at a mid-market price.

The Japanese were reaping the benefits of long-term investment in research and development, and a strong demand for audio equipment in their home markets, but their strongest card was their responsiveness to core consumer wants, such as reliability and standard of finish. Japanese competence in mass production was teamed with new marketing skills. A wide range of models, each marginally higher in price and specification than the last, came and went within a matter of months. Manufacturers spurred consumers to constantly upgrade by spelling out a stream of minor technical advances in detail (these usually figured on the front panel for maximum impact in both the store and the home). ▶▶

## PIONEER SX636

Even at the budget end of the market, Japanese components, such as this Pioneer receiver, sported chunky metal controls, black-glass scales elegantly back-lit in blue or green, and flywheel-loaded tuning knobs which could be spun at a touch. These features gave hi-fi buyers the sense of owning a precision instrument.

▼

date of introduction: **1974, Japan**

size: **48 x 40.5 x 15 cm (19 x 16 x 6 in)**

key features: **combined stereo tuner and amplifier; typical 70s styling**

## AKAI 4000D

Although they faced a challenge from improving cassette decks, moderately priced open-reel tape machines like this one were still in demand in the '70s. The Akai 4000D made a virtue of money-saving simplicity: instead of a complex mechanism to change tape speed, a simple brass sleeve fitted over the capstan (tape-drive spindle) to increase its diameter. It had no power amplifier or speaker, being meant for use with hi-fi equipment. But it did have separate record and playback heads, allowing recording quality to be instantly monitored off the tape, as well as simple track-to-track techniques. Several slightly modified versions, including one with Dolby noise reduction, appeared during the '70s.

▼

date of introduction: **1969, Japan**

size: **33 x 40.5 x 20.5 cm (13 x 16 x 8 in)**

key feature: **two-speed, three head deck**

▲ Sansui was another Japanese brand which gained a big share of the market in the '60s and '70s, with receivers such as this model.

▶

date of introduction: **late 1960s, UK**

designer: **David Gammon**

size: **44 x 42 x 19 cm (17¼ x 16½ x 7½ in)**

key features: **4.5 kg (10 lb) turntable weights; hydraulic speed-control system**

## TRANSCRIPTORS HYDRAULIC REFERENCE TURNTABLE

With its solid aluminium construction, clear acrylic case, and gold-plated brass weights, this would not stand out among some of today's cult turntables, but back in the early '70s it could have landed from another planet. In fact, its maker had supplied props for the 1968 Stanley Kubrick film *2001: A Space Odyssey* (the turntable also appears in Kubrick's *A Clockwork Orange*). Originally designed by engineer David Gammon, by the '70s it was being made by Michell Engineering. The subsequently successful Michell Gyrodec (1982) retained many of the features of the original but also included a disc clamp and suspended sub-chassis.

The Japanese hi-fi of the late '60s and '70s was generally unadventurously styled in chipboard covered in teak or walnut veneer, with satin aluminium front panels screen-printed in black (see p.70). But even budget-priced Japanese components had a feeling of precision and solidity. This was aided by their sheer weight – in the days before plastic mouldings replaced wood and metal frames, and microchips replaced many individual parts.

### New ways with records

In the early '70s cheap, semi-automatic record decks sold complete with cartridge and plinth continued to dominate the budget end of the hi-fi market. Later in the decade such products were replaced by simpler but better-made Japanese decks, such as the best-selling Pioneer PL12D.

With record decks having apparently reached a design plateau, several companies tried to come up with something different. Garrard introduced the Zero 100 deck, which used an articulated pick-up head to reduce the tracking error of the tone-arm as it moved across a record, while others, such as Bang & Olufsen (see p.97), Revox, and Technics (see p.102), introduced parallel-tracking systems in which a servo motor moved the arm across the record surface.

One rather less successful result of Japanese research and design effort was the direct-drive turntable, which integrated the platter into a slow-speed motor rather than driving it via a belt or idler wheel. Quartz-locked direct-drive units sold well for a time, though sound quality was ▶▶

## REGA PLANAR 3

Rega was formed in 1973 by Roy Gandy. The Planar 2 (1975) and Planar 3 turntables with simple belt-drive and glass platters established themselves among the finest budget audiophile products of the day. Later Rega moved ahead in the style game by making plinths in a range of bright colours. In the '80s, the company designed its own ground-breaking tone-arm (shown here), which combined headshell, arm tube, and bearing in a one-piece aluminium casting.

## LINN SONDEK LP12

The LP12, with its heavy balanced belt-driven turntable, low-noise, single-point bearing, and solid suspended sub-chassis, was related to previous designs by AR, Thorens, and Ariston. The turntable was soon seen by many as the "ultimate source" for use with equipment costing a fraction of its price, while Linn expanded into arms, cartridges, speakers, electronics, and its own record label.

▲

date of introduction: **1977, UK**

size: **44.5 x 35.5 x 12 cm (17½ x 14 x 4¾ in)**

key features: **glass platter; belt drive**

▲

date of introduction: **1972, UK**

size: **45 x 34 x 15 cm (17¾ x 13½ x 6 in)**

key features: **suspended sub-chassis; influential brand**

## MARK LEVINSON ML2

Audiophiles focused on how amplifier power ratings did not tell the whole story. The massive ML2 monoblock power amplifier was rated at only twenty-five watts per channel, but sounded far more powerful. The design of its output circuits made them run very hot, necessitating the large cooling fins at the sides.

## NAIM NAP250

Naim's products were unlike most amplifiers of the time: turning conventional marketing wisdom on "perceived value" on its head, almost all controls were eliminated as having a limiting effect on sound quality. The one-piece extruded case shown here is a later version.

▲

date of introduction: **1977, US**

size: **23 x 48 x 56cm (9 x 19 x 22 in)**

key features: **twin monoblock power amplifier; large cooling fins**

▼

date of introduction: **1975, UK**

size: **43 x 30 x 7.5 cm (17 x 11¾ x 3 in)**

key features: **power amplifier; subjectively based design**

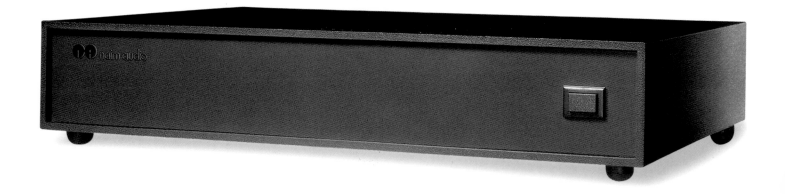

## MERIDIAN 101 CONTROL UNIT/104 TUNER/103 POWER AMP

A key British brand within the late '70s trend towards technical and aesthetic simplicity was Bob Stuart and Alan Boothroyd's Meridian. This range of modular equipment came in neat, dark-brown, slab-like boxes. The focus was on how musical the equipment sounded and the subjective effect of different types of distortion, while the simple control unit had no redundant circuitry that might blur sound detail. Each module was finished in textured enamel with gold lettering. The company went on to develop active loudspeakers and CD players, and was at the leading edge of digital audio and video processing in the '90s.

▶

date of introduction: **1977, UK**

designer: **Alan Boothroyd & Bob Stuart**

size: **14 x 5 x 32 cm (5½ x 2 x 12½ in)**

key features: **modular components; stripped-down design**

generally found wanting by audiophile reviewers, who preferred simpler belt-drive models. But direct-drive decks, such as the successful Technics SL1200 series, had instant start-up which made them ideal for DJ work.

It was not until the late '70s that the hi-fi world came round to the idea that the turntable had a dominant effect on the overall sound of a system. The Scottish company Linn, and its controversial boss Ivor Tiefenbrun, with his slogan "garbage in, garbage out", played a big role in bringing about this reappraisal. Linn's first product, the Sondek LP12 (see p.73), is still made today. This turntable's engineering was above criticism, but its cult following was due as much to its mythologizing and aggressive promotion by dealers and the hi-fi press. Linn – together with British amplifier maker Naim (see opposite) – promoted the belief that a well-balanced system should maintain the pitch accuracy, rhythm, and dynamics of music so that the listener could "sing along with it", rather than simply pursue the traditional aims of tonal neutrality and low distortion.

There was a major shift in much of the hi-fi press away from technical measurements towards more subjective reviewing. This did not take place without acrimony from the old guard, as a 1976 review of the Linn Sondek in *Hi-Fi News* made clear. Mocking the "if it sounds better to me, it is better" approach of the "new wave", the reviewer went on: "This is 'flat-earthing', and whilst it may be fine for some, and even an effective sales tool for others, it has nothing to do with the business of getting good results." The Linn and similar turntables also enhanced their cult status partly by breaching all normal principles of user convenience: they were often tricky to set up and completely non-automatic. ▶▶

◄ Pink Floyd's *Dark Side of the Moon*
(1973) stretched the technical
resources of the Abbey Road studio to
the limits. It went on to be one of the
best-selling rock albums of all time.

# solid state and super groups

Records sales peaked in the 1970s, with over 200 million records and tapes a year sold in the UK alone. Heavy-duty speakers and plenty of power were essential to listen to hard rock supergroups such as Led Zeppelin and Deep Purple, while progressive rock acts like Pink Floyd or Yes also called for absorbed listening with decent sound quality.

In the 1970s musicians made great use of electronic instruments. The Mini-Moog was the first synthesiser portable enough to take on stage, while the Mellotron – still popular early in the decade – was the mechanical forerunner of samplers; each key played a strip of tape with a sound at that key's pitch. There was also the weirdly robotic Vocoder voice-modulated synthesizer. The early '70s saw rapid progress from four-track studio recording through eight, sixteen, twenty-four tracks,

and beyond. Each instrument could now be laid down on a separate track, at different times if need be. For decades, producers had been able to edit together different takes (and the 1972 Yes album *Close to the Edge*, for example, was spliced together with scores of razor-blade edits). But now they had even greater scope to patch over a badly played note or alter the level, equalization, position on the soundstage, or effects on each channel. More time might be spent remixing the record than recording it, though the '80s would see a backlash in favour of simpler, more "authentic" recording techniques.

By the second half of the '70s the pretentiousness of many rock stars had been punctured by the arrival of punk. Hi-fi, too, had its share of iconoclasts in the '70s, who challenged views on turntable and amplifier design.

◄ British heavy metal band Hawkwind's hard rock sound was shot through with sci-fi imagery and '60s psychedelia. The VCS3 synthesizer (played by Del Dettmar, left) was also a key element of Pink Floyd's *Dark Side of the Moon*.

▼ Robert Moog's huge and complex 1960s synthesizers featured in Walter Carlos's successful *Switched on Bach* records. Shown here is his Mini-Moog (1971), the first synthesizer small enough to use on stage.

## GRUNDIG SATELLIT 1000

Grundig was renowned for its line of "world" receivers – radios designed for high-performance reception on short waves. Such listening was a popular hobby and essential for receiving worldwide news broadcasts – much more so than now, when satellite and Internet links have made long-distance communication commonplace. The successful Satellit 1000 had FM, long, and medium waves and no fewer than seventeen wavebands covering frequencies from 1.6 to 30kHz. It had a "drum" tuner so that each small section of the short-wave spectrum was spread over the full length of the tuning scale, making it easy to separate closely packed foreign stations. The Satellit range ran until the mid '90s.

▶

date of introduction: **1972, Germany**

size: **46 x 26 x 13 cm (18 x 10 1/4 x 5 in)**

key features: **seventeen short-wave bands; bandspread tuning**

During the early '70s very light tracking forces (down to less than one gram) and high-compliance moving-magnet cartridges were in fashion. But by the end of the decade the trend was reversed, with the return of moving-coil cartridges and tone-arms that aimed at high rigidity rather than low mass, such as the Grace and Supex products from Japan. Meanwhile the audio world marvelled at the Koetsu cartridges created by Japanese craftsman Yoshiaki Sugano which combined high-purity metals with precious materials like rosewood, ebony and onyx.

### Amplifier arguments

The amplifier scene too saw views polarize between the importance of technical specifications and sound quality. Naim was among the new companies who challenged the thinking of the audio establishment and argued that amplifiers which measured similarly in a testing lab could still sound different. Naim's first products in 1974 (see p.74) were quite unlike either traditional British designs like Quad or most imported models. The company argued that the wide range of controls and filters on such amplifiers was not only unnecessary but actually limited sound quality. Its stripped-down products contradicted marketing principles that

## BANG & OLUFSEN 1900

Bang & Olufsen products had an upmarket niche somewhere between mainstream audio and high-end hi-fi. From the late '60s a series of designs by Jakob Jensen featured receivers as well as turntables and stereo systems that had a sleek, sophisticated, low-slung look in satin aluminium and teak, or black or white. Equipment had uncluttered surfaces and logically laid-out light-touch controls long before these were commonplace. The 1900 receiver of 1976 – with its touch-button pre-set stations and subtle back-lit tuning display – won many awards as well as a place in the Museum of Modern Art, New York.

## ARMSTRONG 626

In the UK, the Armstrong 620 series was a lesser but still stylish example of 1970s industrial design in its use of a recessed plinth to achieve a low cabinet profile. Modular construction allowed the company to offer a range of amplifiers, FM or AM/FM tuners, and receivers. Sadly, the Armstrong brand would, within a few years, finally succumb to competition from imports.

▲

date of introduction: **1976, Denmark**

designer: **Jakob Jensen**

size: **62 x 25 x 6 cm (24½ x 9¾ x 2½ in)**

key features: **sheer styling; touch-button controls**

▼

date of introduction: **1973, UK**

size: **50 x 8 x 29 cm (19¾ x 3 ¼ x 11½ in)**

key features: **modular construction; low-profile cabinet**

stated "the more features the better", making technological and visual minimalism into something of a cult.

While ever-higher amplifier power had became a kind of virility symbol, this was challenged by a new focus on the ability of an amplifier to drive a particular type of loudspeaker. In the US Mark Levinson (see p.74) produced a series of massive amplifiers and pre-amplifiers which were superbly hand-built. In fact, while the US hi-fi industry seemed to have virtually disappeared at the start of the '70s, there was now renewed interest in distinctive equipment produced in small quantities. The launch of the *Stereophile* – in its early years a small, alternative magazine – spurred the development of a "high-end" audio market for auteur products. Later in the decade another, *The Absolute Sound*, gave further impetus to this trend and saw renewed interest in tube amplification. ▶▶

◄

date of introduction: **1968, US**

size: **53 x 32 x 32cm (21 x 12½ x 12½ in)**

key features: **direct/indirect speaker system; electronic equalizer**

◄

date of introduction: **1979, UK**

designer: **Kenneth Grange**

size: **101 x 43 x 56 cm (39¾ x 17 x 22 in)**

key features: **separate bass, mid-range and treble enclosures**

## BOSE 901

Arguing that in a concert much of what the listener hears is indirect sound reflecting off the walls, Bose set out to create the same effect in the domestic setting. All but one of the nine small but full-range drive units face to the rear, away from the listener. An electronic equalizer unit is able to vary bass and treble response to suit different rooms.

## B&W 801

Kenneth Grange became B&W's industrial designer in 1974. His first project was the DM6, which, like the larger 801, had a stepped shape resulting from technical director John Bowers's conviction that the bass and mid-range drive units should be at different distances from the listener. The mid-range cone pioneered the use of Kevlar – a light, strong material used for protective clothing. The 801 was soon widely used as a professional studio monitor.

The Minneapolis company Audio Research, founded in 1970 by William Z. Johnson, was among the first to satisfy this demand for high-end tube equipment. Meanwhile, in the UK, Tim de Paravicini, after working for the Japanese Lux corporation in the mid '70s, spearheaded the design of one of the first amplifiers of the valve renaissance.

### Receiver wisdom

At the start of the '70s almost all FM tuners and receivers still used an analogue tuning knob and scale. But, by the end of the decade, this was being replaced by electronic and then fully digital synthesized tuning, which made it easy to provide push-button selection of pre-set stations, while the absence of a linear tuning scale allowed designers new freedom with front-panel layout – particularly on the new compact components that were becoming available. One notable exception to the box-like sameness of many stereos was Bang & Olufsen. By the late '60s award-winning portable radios like the Beolit had been joined by the designs of Jakob Jensen (see p.79), with their unique and instantly recognizable upmarket style. Bang & Olufsen products found a niche of buyers somewhere between mainstream audio and high-end hi-fi, and its classy image was maintained by the stores chosen to sell it.

### Loudspeaker trends

Small "bookshelf" loudspeakers continued to be popular in many countries and some were capable of increasingly good performance for their ►►

▶

date of introduction: **1973, UK**

size: **30 x 19 x 16 cm (11³/₄ x 7¹/₂ x 6¹/₄ in)**

key features: **birch-ply cabinet; KEF-made drive units**

## ROGERS LS3/5A

The BBC's LS3/5A design was originally meant for monitoring in outside-broadcast trucks, but it was soon taken up for home hi-fi. The LS3/5A produced a surprising amount of bass for its size, as well as a clear and accurate mid- and high-frequency response. It was produced by Rogers and several other manufacturers, remained in production until 1998, and has recently been revived. Rogers had also had a name for good-value amplifiers since the '50s, while Jim Rogers's JR149 speaker (1977) was a unique design using a near-cylindrical non-resonant aluminium enclosure.

size and price. Britain was still the focus of much technological development in speakers in the 1970s, including the use of computer modelling to optimize crossover design, and materials technology such as new plastics for speaker cone surrounds. KEF (founded by Raymond Cooke in 1961) was a case in point; and while it marketed loudspeakers such as the long-running Coda model under its own name, its drive units were used in many other makers' speakers. US companies too, like Infinity and KLH, drew on aerospace and other advanced technologies in the use of new plastics for speaker design, and the development of "active" speakers (which incorporate their own tailored amplification as a way of improving performance).

From modest beginnings in Worthing, England, Bowers and Wilkins grew into an internationally successful loudspeaker business. Kenneth Grange, a founding partner of the leading international Pentagram design consultancy, became B&W's industrial designer in 1974, beginning a long-lasting relationship with the company. As well as the large floor-standing B&W 801 (see p.81), launched in 1979, the smaller DM (Domestic Monitor) series was successful throughout the decade.

The BBC's design department also helped the reputation of British loudspeakers during the decade with its small LS3/5A design which was originally meant for monitoring in outside-broadcast trucks. The ▶▶

## KOSS PRO 4AA

The detailed binaural sound – feeding left and right channels separately to each ear – provided by stereo headphones added to the prog rock experience. John Koss developed his first stereo headphones using old military headsets, but sales didn't take off until Koss had persuaded hi-fi companies to fit headphone jacks. Typical of the '70s, the PRO 4AA had large ear-cups that fitted over the ears with a cushioned seal.

## SENNHEISER HD414

The German company Sennheiser's headphones were lighter, stylish, and gave excellent sound. Hugely successful, their open-backed design pointed the way to Sony's miniature Walkman phones. The bright yellow earpads hinted at how primary colour would challenge the sober black-and-silver look of hi-fi in later years.

▲

date of introduction: **1970, US**

key feature: **closed over-ear design**

▶

date of introduction: **1972, Germany**

key feature: **open-back ear-pad design**

## STAX SR-X

In the opinion of many reviewers the finest headphones in the world have come from the Japanese company Stax. After making microphones and cartridges in the 1950s, Stax introduced the first-ever electrostatic "ear speakers", the SR1, in 1960. Like electrostatic speakers, these used the principle of an almost weightless diaphragm suspended between parallel electrified grids. The SR-X shown here appeared in 1970. The matching SRD-7 unit provides the power for the headphones as well as switching between phones and speakers. Later models, such as the Sigma (1977), Lambda (1982), and top-end Omega, consolidated the company's reputation.

larger Spendor BC1 was also used as a BBC monitor, as well as being a highly regarded speaker in the domestic market for over 20 years.

"Omnidirectional" speakers like the Sonab from Sweden were a largely unsuccessful early '70s attempt to make the stereo effect less dependent on the listener's location. But Bose (see p.81) developed designs that directed sound away from the listener so that it was reflected off the walls of the room, adding ambience to the sound. Other companies developed large "sub-woofers" to add deep bass to existing speaker systems. At the time this was mainly a technique for no-compromise hi-fi enthusiasts, but the principle is now widely used to add bass to the small "satellite" surround-sound speakers used in many home cinema systems.

### Personal listening

Stereo headphones had become popular with hi-fi enthusiasts as a cheap alternative to loudspeakers or as a way of listening privately to music at high sound levels. They were first developed at the end of the '50s just as transistor radios were beginning to popularize personal listening; John Koss, for example, built a set of stereo headphones using old military headsets fitted with tiny speakers and padding from flight helmets. The Koss brand (see p.83) became synonymous with stereo headphones in the '60s and '70s. Most early headphones had large, fairly heavy, padded cups fitting right over the ears, but the German company Sennheiser's headphones pioneered a lighter-on-the-ear style. Hugely successful ▶▶

▶

date of introduction: **1970, Japan**

key feature: **electrostatic design**

**Panasonic.**
just slightly ahead of our time.

## SANSUI QUAD SYSTEM

By 1972 everyone was talking about quadraphony, but a damaging formats battle had begun. Some companies backed Columbia's SQ matrix system, others RCA's Quadradisc CD4 (developed by JVC), which used a high-frequency sub-carrier to carry the two extra channels. These two scored an early advantage over quad tape systems and QS (a different matrix system backed by Sansui). Under these conditions, getting consumers to invest in all-new equipment was difficult – the Sansui add-on system (bottom right) with two extra speakers was one option. The Panasonic music system (top) may have been "slightly ahead of our time" but it also included the ill-fated eight-track cartridge player.

▼

date of introduction: **1970s, Japan**

key feature: **quadraphonic speakers; add·on system**

▲ Panasonic quadrophonic system with 8-track cartridge player.

in the following decade, their open-backed design (patented in the late '60s) pointed the way to Sony's miniature Walkman headphones. However, by common consent the finest headphones in the world came from the Japanese company Stax. After making microphones and cartridges in the 1950s, Stax introduced the first ever electrostatic headphones in 1960 (see p.84).

## Four channels fail

Now that surround sound features in many homes, it is easy to forget that quadraphonic (four-channel) discs and systems failed totally when they were launched at the start of the '70s. They did not aim for surround sound in quite the way we understand it now, but, to create the illusion of being in a concert hall, used rear speakers to give depth as well as width.

In what looked like a re-run of the 33/45rpm battle of the late '40s, Columbia (and EMI in the UK) backed the SQ matrix system while RCA's Quadradisc used the JVC-developed CD4 system, which used a high-frequency sub-carrier to carry the two extra channels. These two scored an early advantage over quad tape systems and QS (a different matrix system backed by Sansui). But, as often happens when consumers are presented with a choice of competing formats, in the end they steered clear of all of them, and all formats had disappeared by the late '70s. All of the systems had some technical shortcomings, while none had a good variety of software available. Furthermore, the public had to be ▶▶

## ADVENT 201

Henry Kloss founded Advent in 1967. This was one of the first companies to produce a cassette deck that seriously threatened open reel for hi-fi. The key development was the introduction of Dolby noise reduction (see p.90). It was Kloss who helped persuade Ray Dolby to introduce a simplified "B" consumer version of the Dolby "A" noise reduction system, and the 201 was one of the first cassette decks to incorporate it.

▶

date of introduction: **1971, US**

size: **35.5 x 24 x 11.5cm (14 x 9½ x 4½ in)**

key feature: **early hi-fi deck; Dolby "B" noise reduction**

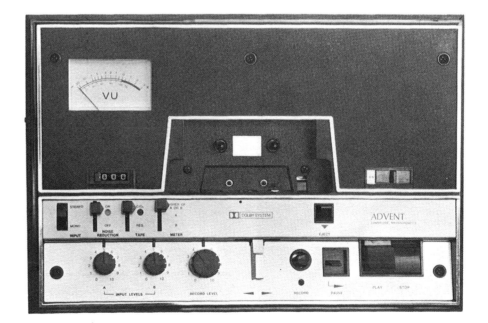

## YAMAHA TC800D

Compared to his earlier designs, Mario Bellini's work became more angular in the '70s; this has been linked to his use of polystyrene cut with a hot wire as a model-making medium. Cassette decks, which at first were mostly top-loaders like the Advent opposite, flirted with sloping panels before settling on the front-loading style (see for example page 91). Bellini's striking wedge design for Yamaha in fact allowed for two angles of operation through a pivoting support underneath. It also differs from most high quality decks in being able to run on batteries as well as mains current.

▲

date of introduction: **1975, Japan**

size: **31x31x13cm (12¼x12¼x5in)**

key features: **angled design; battery or mains operation**

► By the 1970s hi-fi had become a mainstream purchase and several new magazines catered for this non-specialist market. By the end of the decade, though, video was competing with audio for consumer spending.

## WEGA CONCEPT 51K

Wega was a design-conscious German company – in the '60s, for example it had engaged Verner Panton to design a stereo system (see p.9). The Concept adopts the wide, horizontal style of many '70s stereos but the matt-black contours have a distinctly '80s feel. The record player arm can be viewed through the clear plastic segment in the lid. The Concept was designed by Hartmut Esslinger, whose design consultancy (helped partly by Sony's marketing skills after it took over Wega) grew into a global creative network. This was renamed *frogdesign* in 1982 and opened offices in California (winning a major contract with Apple Computers) and in Japan.

▶

date of introduction: **1975, Germany**

designer: **Hartmut Esslinger**

size: **84 x 40 x 12 cm (33 x 15³/₄ x 4³/₄ in)**

key feature: **stereo system with record player, radio, and cassette recorder**

the Walkman, developed at the tail end of the '70s, was an enormously successful product for which there had apparently been no demand).

Using the briefing received, in-house or consulting designers would work up rough sketches of several alternative shapes and styles. Scale models cut out of foam plastic and "exploded" views of the construction would be prepared, to get first reactions from sales and production departments. There was always pressure to simplify manufacturing processes or reduce the number of parts wherever possible. For a chosen design, detailed drawings and an accurate non-working model could then be prepared, and work might start on the tooling required to make the product (which could take months for a complex plastic moulding). While this was happening, discussions would continue about issues such as the colour and applied graphics of the finished product.

With these points resolved, final engineering drawings could be completed, and costs and production and marketing plans confirmed. But there could still be a trial production run to test consumer response or to iron out quality-control problems before full-scale manufacture began.

A 1970s designer was using techniques that would have been familiar to a practitioner from the '50s or '60s. But all this was about to change: during the '80s and '90s computer-aided design and manufacture would affect not only the design process but also the kinds of design that could be produced cost-effectively.

## BANG & OLUFSEN
## 4002/4400

A Beomaster 4400 receiver with typical Bang & Olufsen slide-rule type controls is partnered with a 4002 turntable with miniature parallel-tracking tone-arm driven by electronic servo control. Such arms aim to avoid the distortion which can be caused by conventionally pivoted tone-arms, by following the straight-line motion of the cutting head used to make the original master disc.

## BRIONVEGA TOTEM RR130

A Bellini stereo system for Brionvega. A discreet white cube when closed, the loudspeaker boxes swing out at the rear or can be lifted off altogether and spaced apart for better stereo separation. The central unit has neat recessed controls.

▲

date of introduction: **1974-7, Denmark**

designer: **Jakob Jensen**

size (4400): **57.5 x 28 x 9.5cm (22³/₄ x 11 x 3³/₄ in)**

key features: **parallel-tracking arm**

▼

date of introduction: **1971, Italy**

designer: **Mario Bellini**

size: **52.5 x 52 x 51 cm (20³/₄ x 20¹/₂ x 20 in)**

key features: **Italian high-style design; multi-purpose speakers**

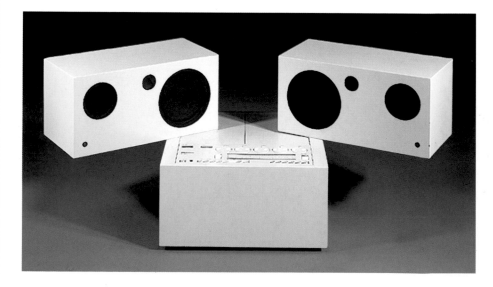

▲ After the success of the first
Walkman (see p.122), new versions
such as the splashproof "Sports"
model were constantly being developed
during the '80s.

# 1980-1989 **digital**delivery

▲

date of introduction: **1982-3, Netherlands**

size: **32 x 25.5 x 7.5cm (12½ x 10 x 3 in)**

key features: **top-loading; early CD player**

◀

date of introduction: **1982-3, Japan**

size: **35.5 x 32.5 x 10.5cm
(14 x 12¾ x 4¼in)**

key features: **front-loading; many
programming features**

## PHILIPS CD100

This and the Sony model below were among the first CD players to be widely available. Twenty years on, the top-loading elegance of the Philips has worn well, although, as with cassette decks, front-loaders won the day. The Philips design was also used by Marantz, and several audiophile brands produced refined versions.

## SONY CDP101

The powered front-loading drawer soon became almost universal, being more suited to stacking systems. It also had more sophisticated track-searching and programming than the Philips. The black fascia is typically '80s, as is the word "digital", which rapidly became a sales buzzword.

The 1980s saw the compact disc (CD) bring new standards of quality into mass-market audio, but video was competing strongly for consumer spending. Meanwhile the Walkman changed the image of personal audio.

### The birth of CD

Digital technology not only provided a totally new music format, but also affected how music was recorded in the studio. The end of the '70s had seen rapid progress: the first digital studio recordings (released on analogue LP) had been made in the US in 1977, and Philips had given prototype demonstrations of CDs the following year. In addition, Sony produced equipment that allowed digital recordings to be made on a Betamax VCR.

CDs are made by using a laser to burn a spiral of microscopic pits (representing the digital data) on to a master disc, which can then be used to press copies for sale. A laser is also used in the CD player to scan the disc and retrieve the data. All of these developments depended on "sampling" an analogue music signal tens of thousands of times a second and defining it as a stream of digital data, which could then be recorded or copied many times with no loss of quality. In 1979, the magazine *High Fidelity* asked: "Will the digital disc really take over the music reproduction field, or even the audiophile corner of it, in the next decade or two?" They were soon to find out. Philips and Sony began a joint development programme to improve the CD before its launch in Japan in 1982 and a world roll-out the following year. ▶▶

▲

date of introduction: **1986, US**

size: **42 x 30 x 11.5cm (16½ x 12 x 4½ in)**

key features: **audiophile CD player; tube-output circuits**

### CALIFORNIA AUDIO LABS (CAL) TEMPEST

It was not long before audiophile companies such as CAL took CD mechanisms meant for mainstream players and matched them with high-quality tweaked electronics. It was perhaps inevitable that eventually someone would come up with the apparently bizarre concept of the Tempest – a CD player that combined the latest digital-to-analogue micro-chips with good old-fashioned tubes in the analogue output circuits. But, whatever the effect on sound quality, it probably helped to make the CD more acceptable to the growing band of enthusiasts for retro technology.

## TECHNICS SL10

Technics was among the first to produce smaller hi-fi components such as its Concise series of 1979 (see also p.119). As electronic technology had shrunk, much of the space inside conventionally sized amplifiers and tuners was now redundant. At the same time, the very neatness and novelty of microsystems could command a higher price tag. But, with vinyl still predominant, the size of the record deck was a limiting factor. Technics' ingenious response was the SL10, with dimensions the same as an LP sleeve and a tiny parallel-tracking arm mounted on the lid. So precise was the lid design that the deck would play vertically as well as horizontally.

▶

date of introduction: **1980, Japan**

size: **31.5 x 31.5 x 9 cm
(12½ x 12½ x 3½ in)**

key features: **small size; parallel tracking tone-arm**

CDs were launched with the promise of "perfect sound forever" and so were bound to cause controversy. Early demonstrations in the media exaggerated the durability of the disc itself. But the format did overcome many of the problems of LPs and cassettes, and, in mass-market terms, it was a big advance in both sound quality and convenience, with quick access, search, and programming of tracks, as well as over seventy minutes' interrupted play.

Classical music listeners mostly took to CDs with enthusiasm, praising their quiet background and lack of obvious distortion on choral works or opera. But for others, CDs were far from perfect: compared with the "warmth" of vinyl, the sound was widely claimed to be harsh and uninvolving in ways which were hard to pin down. Hi-fi journalists were also unhappy: turntable, arm, and cartridge combinations could be endlessly debated but what could be said about an apparently non-adjustable black box? In the US *The Absolute Sound* was highly critical of the CD in the early days, while some turntable makers ran advertising presenting the CD as a no-hope format that would fail just as quadraphonic sound had done in the '70s.

The CDs themselves, with their rainbowed silver surfaces, were regarded with some awe, especially in the early years, when they tested plastics technology to the limit: pressing facilities were scarce and the

▲

date of introduction: **1981, Germany**

size: **44 x 37 x 14 cm (17½ x 14½ x 5½ in)**

key features: **low-mass tone-arm; fine-speed control**

## DUAL CS 505

Vinyl was still big business for much of the decade. Dual had been making gramophone motors since the 1900s (its name is said to have come from motors that worked off either spring-wound or electric power) and its precision-made automatic players and changers were steady sellers. This model looks unexceptional, but it became the budget deck to have in 1980s Britain. It had an integrated deck with low-mass, gimbal-mounted arm, foolproof cueing, and automatic stop, and its speed could be finely adjusted. Some versions had strobo-scopic markings on the platter rim.

reject rate was high. Few would have imagined that such apparently precious objects would, in ten years or so, be given away free with magazines. Sadly their small size limited the scope for sleeve art, which had thrived since the rock LPs of the '60s.

The word "digital" acquired the aura of modernity just as "transistor" had twenty-five years earlier, and was applied to all kinds of analogue equipment, including speakers and headphones. At first player prices were high, but as CDs became popular these fell. By about 1987 LP sales were declining dramatically and CD singles were appearing for the first time.

It was not long before the audiophile hi-fi industry started trying to resolve what it saw as the inadequacies of CD playback. These were linked to how faithfully the analogue signal could be retrieved. While the Philips/Sony CD specification limited the number of digital bits and the sampling rate used to encode the music signal, sophisticated "over-sampling" and interpolation techniques were developed to extend the format's practical capabilities. Audiophile companies took CD drives destined for mainstream players and matched them with tweaked electronics while separately-housed, high-spec DACs (digital-to-analogue converters) were also introduced.

As well as in the home, the CD was ideal for the car, where its track access and programmability helped it score over the cassette player. ▶▶

◄ As pop's focus shifted away from rock to dance and from concert to club, DJs became stars in their own right. Turntables, such as these Technics models, were part of the act.

# synthetic sounds

In the 1980s digital technology changed the way people listened to music: CDs were much more convenient than vinyl LPs. But digital also changed the way music itself was created: pop began to be programmable. Sequencers and more sophisticated synthesizers made musicians less dependent than ever on acoustically produced sounds, spawning successful electro-pop bands such as Depeche Mode, Human League, and the Pet Shop Boys. The Australian Fairlight sampler was the first to digitize real sounds instead of trying to produce them electronically, and by the end of the '80s samplers were widely used.

Futuristic electronic beats – above all from the German band Kraftwerk – also inspired club DJs and producers to remix them with elements of rap, jazz, and dub reggae. In the process, they reshaped dance

music in a black idiom, kick-starting a succession of styles including hip-hop, house, and techno. DJs became stars in their own right; turntables no longer just played records but became a part of the act as DJs created new sounds by spinning the decks by hand. By the end of the '80s many of these initially radical styles had crossed over into mainstream pop.

Brian Eno had been a guru of avant-garde pop in the '70s; his first self-styled "ambient" record, *Music for Airports* (1978), was meant, he said, to "induce calm and a space to think". Here again, synthesizers and samplers provided new possibilities for shaping sounds and creating an all-enveloping sonic environment. Alongside techno, ambient would have a continuing effect on dance styles as well as on "electronica" compositions meant mainly for home listening.

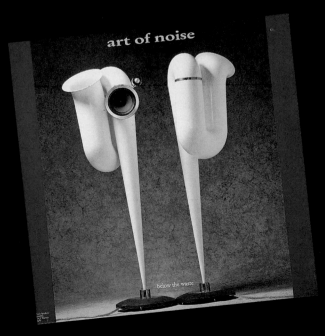

▲ Experimental German band Kraftwerk had made their name in the '70s but wcrc a big influence on '80s electro-pop bands as well as on hip-hop artists such as Afrika Bambaataa.

◄ The Art of Noise were an early '80s techno-pop group centred on arranger/producer Anne Dudley. The sleeve of their 1989 album featured Bowers & Wilkins's Emphasis speakers.

Cassette players were, by the '80s, included in most cars, but the CD combined with 1980s trends in street style to push car audio to new heights of quality and power. Simple radio-cassettes were upstaged by customized component systems featuring remote-controlled CD changers, high-output amplification, and massive speaker installations.

## Vinyl lives on

At first the limited choice of music on CD meant that even early adopters needed to keep their record-playing equipment. But in a few years it was clear that vinyl's days as a mass-market music medium were numbered.

As attitudes to the CD polarized in the hi-fi press, the hands-on ritual of turntables became attractive to many. CD, while convenient, seemed to offer very little scope for the traditional hi-fi pleasures of fine-tuning and experiment. As budget-priced record decks began to disappear, attention focused on the audiophile turntable designs of the '70s, though one short-lived design (recently revived) tried to use the laser-scanning principles of a CD player as a wear-free way of "reading" the grooves on a vinyl disc.

Vinyl continued to be a mainstay of the DJ and dance-club scene, as it still is today, and its alternative image was heightened by the issue of limited-edition pressings of both new avant-garde and old rock material.

## New cults

While Far Eastern electronics (by now mostly made in lower-waged Korea, China, or Malaysia, rather than Japan) continued to dominate the ▶▶

### RADFORD STA25 SERIES 4

In the '50s and '60s Arthur Radford built a classic series of amplifiers and control units as well as loudspeakers. The original STA25 appeared in 1965, when most makers (including Radford) were switching over to solid-state designs. Following the tube revival at the end of the '70s, such was its reputation that it was chosen for a commemorative Series 4 edition.

### CONRAD-JOHNSON PREMIER THREE

The conrad-johnson Premier Three pre-amplifier (1983) was described in *The Absolute Sound* as among the finest-sounding equipment of the decade. In tune with the times, its design philosophy centred on subjective assessment and emotional responses to how music sounded. The sturdy handles show the close link to professional equipment design.

◀

date of introduction: **1984, UK**

size: **35.5 x 27.5 x 21.5 cm**
**(14 x 10³/₄ x 8¹/₂ in)**

key feature: **key '60s valve design, revived in the '80s**

▲

date of introduction: **1983, US**

size: **48.5 x 12.5 x 30 cm (19 x 5 x 12 in)**

key features: **high-spec components; professional-style rack mounting**

## KRELL KSA 80

Though Far Eastern audio dominated
the mass market, several new
companies entered the high-end
sector with some success. While
some focused on tube technology,
others harnessed the brute power of
high-current solid-state designs. One
such company was Krell, founded by
Dan D'Agostino in 1980 (and named
after the super-race in the '50s sci-fi
movie *Forbidden Planet*). Some new
loudspeakers proved hard for
apparently powerful solid-state
amplifiers to drive, but Krell's first
product, the KSA100 stereo power
amplifier, was up to the task and,
after it proved unexpectedly
successful, a number of smaller
versions followed, including the
KSA80 of 1987. At the front is a
PAM7 pre-amplifier.

▶

date of introduction: **1987, US**

designer: **Dan D'Agostino**

size: **48.5 x 47 x 23 cm (19 x 18½ x 9 in)**

key feature: **high-power solid-state design**

mass market for hi-fi separates and package systems, several new companies entered the no-compromise high-end market with some success.

There was a trend for heavy-duty amplifiers whose technology (though solid-state) ran very hot, and large metal cooling fins or fans were needed to disperse the heat, as the models by Krell (see left) and Mark Levinson (see p.74) illustrate. Levinson lost control of his brand name to another company in the early '80s but went on to found the Cello brand, which, throughout most of the '80s and '90s, made even more expensive and exclusive equipment, including customized home theatre systems.

The late '70s renaissance of valve amplifiers for a niche market continued during the '80s, with classic equipment from the period including amplifiers from Audio Research and Radford (see p.106). There was also new interest in collecting and using vintage equipment from the '50s and '60s.

But whether favouring valve or high-end solid-state, by the end of the decade designers were going out of their way to produce equipment that also looked distinctive, adopting either an over-engineered military/industrial look, or one of elaborate simplicity, or a quirkily postmodern use of colour and form. Consumer electronics shows in Las Vegas or Milan could now be as much as about fashion as technology.

Some moderately priced hi-fi separates steered a course between the mainstream and the esoteric. One of the most successful makers was NAD. Founded in 1973 by a European dealers' consortium, the brand was helped to take off in the late '70s by restructuring and design input ▶▶

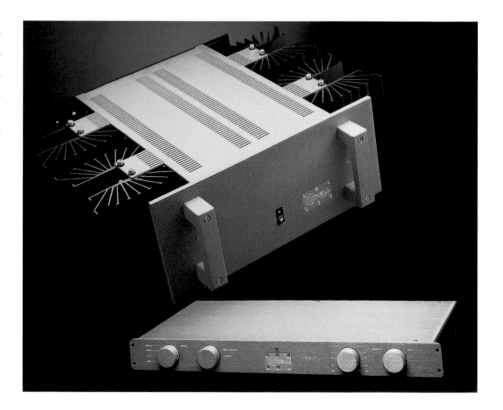

## NAKAMICHI 1000 ZXL

It was the Japanese company
Nakamichi that set the standard for
what could be achieved in cassette
decks. One of Nakamichi's
achievements was to fit a third tape
head into the very limited space
available at the edge of the cassette.
Using separate heads for recording
and playback meant the design of each
could be optimized and recordings
could be immediately monitored off
the tape – a benefit that had been
lost in the switch from open-reel
tape-recorders. As tape-coating
technology developed, Nakamichi also
pioneered an automatic calibration
system, which ensured the best
possible results from different types
of tape. This was the first model to
have the system.

▲

date of introduction: **1980, Japan**

size: **52.5 x 25.5 x 32cm (20³/₄ x 10¹/₄ x 12¹/₂ in)**

key features: **three tape heads; tape-calibration computer**

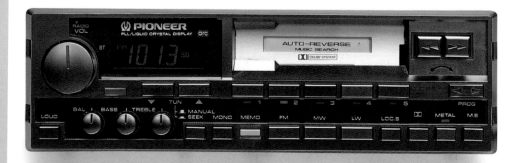

▲ Pioneer car radio cassette player;
the black finish and digital display is
typical of 1980s design.

◄

date of introduction: **1983, UK**

size: **27x19x18cm (10³/₄ x 7¹/₂ x 7 in)**

key features: **big-selling small-box design; low price**

## WHARFEDALE DIAMOND

Many Wharfedale products could have featured in this book. Back in the 1950s, the company, along with Goodmans, specialized in drive units and plans for DIY constructors to use to build their own speaker cabinets. Then, in the '70s, almost every entry-level hi-fi system seemed to feature a pair of teak-clad Wharfedale Dentons or Lintons. But it was an unassuming small-box speaker launched in 1982 that became something of a legend. Selling over five million in various versions, it also acquired something earlier Wharfedale products rarely had: credibility with fickle hi-fi critics. A reminder that one of the aims of design is constructing and maintaining a demand for the product.

from the US and the 3020 amplifier in particular sold in large numbers. The matt charcoal-coloured fascias and restrained graphics set NAD apart from most other budget hi-fi equipment.

### Home taping becomes an issue

As cassette decks and tapes continued to develop in quality, it was above all the Japanese company Nakamichi (see p.109) which set the standard for what could be achieved from the originally low-fi cassette, producing a series of high-quality decks, including the 1000 ZXL and Dragon.

Nineteen eighty-seven saw the launch in Japan of Digital Audio Tape (DAT). With tapes about half the size of a normal cassette, and a recording system using rapidly spinning tape heads like those in a VCR, DAT offered digital-quality sound as well as more rapid track access. But, though it was planned as a high-quality replacement for cassettes in the home, DAT was adopted mainly by professional users.

Such improvements in recording quality continued to worry record companies concerned about lost sales, especially as many stereo systems now included twin cassette decks to simplify copying. In the '80s there were continued calls for levies on cassette prices, and "spoiler" signals on recordings to inhibit copying. But amid widespread criticism that such systems had a significant effect on sound quality (quite apart from the rights and wrongs of home taping), the industry backed down.

### Loudspeakers large and small

Speakers for mainstream budget hi-fi systems continued to be small-box types, and the Wharfedale Diamond was a successful example. ►►

◄ David Wilson's pyramidal WATT monitor (1986) was based on one he designed for use in his recording company. The matched "Puppy" floor-standing bass unit followed in 1988.

▼

date of introduction: **1985, US**

size: **145 x 76 x 9 cm (57 x 30 x 3½ in)**

key feature: **full-range ribbon design**

## APOGEE SCINTILLA

Ribbon loudspeakers (which produce sound by a vibrating tensioned metal ribbon in a magnetic field) had their supporters in the '50s, and Quad and Stanley Kelly produced classic high-frequency ribbon designs. Three decades later the US company Apogee adopted the technique for a full-range model, using a ribbon for the bass as well as middle and higher frequencies. The first model was large and extremely expensive, with ribbons over 1.8m (6ft) long; the rather smaller Scintilla followed in 1985. In this open-panel design, tall and slim, the bass element in the centre has an area equivalent to eight conventional 30cm (12in) bass speakers; the narrow mid/high-frequency ribbon is on the right. Smaller models using conventional cone speakers for deep bass followed, before the company closed in 1998.

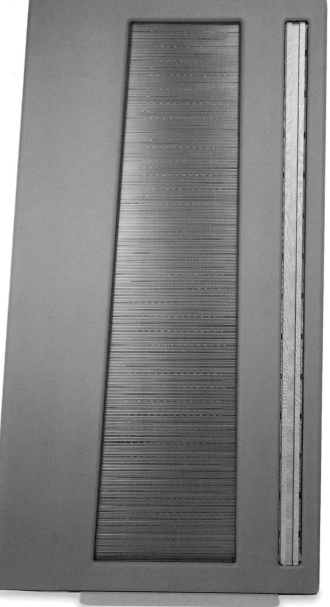

# rap and the boom box

Combining a cassette recorder and a radio was an obvious step, but the low-powered mono models of the '70s had little credibility. By the end of the decade, though, more sensitive technology meant that stereo broadcasts could be received. Small speakers with good bass and high-capacity cells powering multi-watt amplification were developed, while twin-deck models allowed easy copying. All these factors led to products that were bigger (which enhanced their status value) and to which stereo speakers gave stylish symmetry.

Meanwhile new trends in street culture that harked back to the massive "sound systems" of the Jamaican reggae scene spotted the possibilities of the cord-free high-powered sound on offer. Teenagers in New York's Harlem and the Bronx, bored with '70s disco, began taping and mixing bits of black funk records. When

MCs started adding their own chanted vocal lines, the style became rap, a new sound which appealed to a club audience as well as to boom-box breakdancers in the streets and parks. Rap became part of a whole hip-hop sub-culture with its own dress code and graffiti art, while the dance routines were picked up by electro-funk pop artists such as Michael Jackson and Prince.

Major record companies were at first wary of rap acts, which they saw as too provocative for the mainstream market. There were no rap acts at the 1985 Live Aid fund-raising concert or on MTV in its early years. This left the field open to independent labels like Def Jam, which released acts like LL Cool J, Run DMC, and Public Enemy. But, by the '90s, rap had been commodified into corporate white pop, with even acts like the Spice Girls influenced by rap stylings.

◄ The stereo radio cassette allowed performers, rappers, and DJs to take their music and dance to the streets. The trend for breakdancing first began in New York in the early 1980s, but it quickly became a phenomenon throughout the world.

◄◄ ▼ Stereo radio recorders like these, often called "ghetto blasters" or "boom boxes", were intended to be very loud and very big.

The wood or wood-effect veneers of previous decades gave way to the widespread use of a matt-black or textured "black ash" finish which matched the look of other audio products.

One long-awaited event of the '80s was the replacement of the long-running 1957 Quad ESL electrostatic loudspeaker (see p.39) with a new model, the ESL63. But, despite good reviews, the new model has not retained the cult status of the original. In fact, the general revival of interest in vintage audio extended to speaker technology. Horn loudspeakers, which had been popular thirty years earlier, again attracted audiophiles as their high efficiency meant that they could be used with low-powered tube amplifiers, while the US company Apogee (founded in 1981) adopted another technique from the 1950s to produce a full-range ribbon loudspeaker design (see p.111).

Such extravagant technology also allowed – or in some cases required – designers to move away from rectangular wood-veneered boxes. High-end speakers became architectural, monolithic objects finished in high-gloss paint, perforated metal, or exotic woods, whose taller forms combined high performance with a strikingly modern design presence and at the same time took up relatively little floor space.

## High-end trends

Increasingly, high-end retailers operated consultancy-style businesses with private listening rooms for their clients. The upper end of the audio market was becoming ever more subject to the whims of fashion, and was often reviewed in the same colourful and opinionated style as an action movie or a performance car. Critics wielded considerable power in deciding which brands were in and which were out – the latter often being the formerly revered products of the '60s and early '70s. ▶▶

◀

date of introduction: **1980, Canada**

size: **36 x 47.5 x 15 cm (14¼ x 18¾ x 6 in)**

key features: **suspended sub-chassis design; record clamp**

### ORACLE DELPHI

Oracle grew from the experience of a high-end dealer, Marcel Riendeau in Quebec, Canada. The record is clamped to a sonically inert platter, while the sub-chassis is supported by three pillars which absorb vibrations and prevent resonances. The Mk IV version of 1989 is shown.

### MUSICAL FIDELITY A1

Clarinettist Antony Michaelson was in at the start of the tube revival in hi-fi before founding Musical Fidelity in 1982, and focusing on solid-state designs. The A1 was an integrated amplifier in a sleek minimalist case selling for an affordable £250.

▼

date of introduction: **1985, UK**

size: **41 x 25 x 7 cm (16 x 9¾ x 2¾ in)**

key feature: **slim "Class A" design**

## AKAI MIDI SYSTEM

By the mid '80s, the floor-standing rack system was displaced by successively smaller designs, one of which was the "midi" system. Based on the usual width of a CD deck, it was still possible by careful design to incorporate a vinyl turntable with a normal pivoted tone-arm. As well as a CD player, this typical midi system has twin cassette decks (for easy copying), graphic equaliser type tone controls and digital displays. The components are separate but one-piece units often adopted a similar 'stacked' look. The speakers, too, have shrunk in scale.

▼

date of introduction: **1980s, Japan**

size: **45 x 35 x 45 cm (17½ x 13½ x 17½ in)**

key features: **twin cassette decks; slider equalizer controls**

and function keys were replaced by light-touch buttons operating servo motors or solid-state switching, and this also allowed remote control to become a common feature. Blue or green fluorescent or liquid-crystal displays replaced the red LEDs and analogue scales of the '70s.

### A parade of portables

Sony's Walkman personal cassette player was one of the great success stories of the decade and said a great deal about its culture (see p.121). Launched in 1979, the Walkman was no great leap forward technologically, though it came with lightweight headphones that, for their size, gave previously unheard-of bass response. The concept also emphasized the new importance ergonomics would have on small personal equipment. Though expensive at first, (about $100 or $200) the Walkman quickly became hugely popular. Dozens of even smaller and more stylish models followed, while the word became the accepted global generic for any personal cassette player. It was followed in 1985 by the first Discman personal CD player and in the 1990s by MiniDisc and web-music versions.

Another masterly marketing concept from Sony in the '80s was the My First Sony range of radios and cassette players for children. Chunky and robust in primary, toy-like colours, they not only appealed to parents but presumably helped to instil brand loyalty at an early age.

In the '80s the stereo radio recorder largely replaced the mono '70s models. The product in fact divided into distinguishable sub-categories. ▶▶

## TECHNICS LA MINI SÉRIE

Technics was among the first to market small home systems in an upmarket way (the French name is an unusual touch for a Japanese product). Some in the industry thought audio buyers would always link size with power and performance, and with vinyl still a significant seller, the size of conventional record decks was also a limiting factor. Technics' SL10 deck (see p. 102) was an elegant solution to this problem, but in the event the problem disappeared as CD and cassette became the only music formats that mainstream buyers wanted.

►

date of introduction: **1980, Japan**

size: **32 x 27 x 30 cm (12½ x 10½ x 11¾ in)**

key feature: **early compact stacking system**

# NOBODY EVER OFFERED YOU LESS FOR YOUR MONEY.

▼ As portables grew more powerful and in-home units grew smaller, the distinction between them became blurred. On this Sanyo portable, the speaker units can be unhooked and spaced apart for a better stereo effect.

date of introduction: **1983, Japan**

size: **50 x 28 x 13 cm (19³/₄ x 11 x 5 in)**

key features: **stereo; soft-touch controls; Dolby**

date of introduction: **1979, Japan**

size: **13.5 x 9 x 3 cm (5¹/₄ x 3¹/₂ x 1¹/₄ in)**

key features: **first Walkman; small on-ear phones**

## SHARP GF8989

By the '80s, more sensitive radio technology and improved speaker design meant that stereo (rather than mono) radio cassette recorders became the norm. They ranged from huge, flashy "boom boxes", which became a familiar part of street culture, to small and stylish fashion items, and "compo" portables with detachable speakers. The common factor was the stereo speakers, which gave the design a stylish symmetry. This model is typical of the mid '80s with its analogue tuning and power-assisted "soft-touch" cassette controls. Metal cassette tapes were also a new development.

## SONY WALKMAN TPS-L2

The Walkman was an early outcome of Sony's integration of product innovation, design, and marketing. This first model used a proven voice-recorder mechanism, but the key advance was the lightweight headphones, which gave unheard-of bass response for their size. The next model, the WM2, was a leap forward in design terms, with a belt holster, surface-mounted controls, and a coloured case. Hundreds of variants followed, including solar-powered and water-resistant yellow "sports" models (see p.98). The "on-ear" headphones gave way to even smaller in-ear types such as those shown on page 132.

There were huge, flashy "boom boxes" or "ghetto blasters" (see p.112), as well as "compo" (component) portables with detachable speaker boxes, a cross between a portable and a fixed home system.

## Audio in the designer eighties

Buyers may think they choose a brand of stereo on rational grounds – because it has a reliable reputation for example – but a brand can have an enormous symbolic power of its own. By the aspirational 1980s, consumers were becoming increasingly skilled at using visible branding to say something about themselves – prosperous, dependable, cutting-edge, funky – as well as at decoding the brands they saw other people with. In the same way marketing teams were using sophisticated demographic data to define the target buyer when drawing up a design brief.

Meanwhile a new, more individualist consumer was served by lifestyle magazines and the increasingly sophisticated design of retail outlets. Indeed, some shops were virtually indistinguishable from the new design museums that displayed mass-produced consumer products like works of art.

In response, European companies like Philips and Grundig began alliances with companies such as Alessi and Porsche, or designers such as Philippe Starck, though the designs they came up with probably mattered less than the use of their names. Japanese makes, in contrast, usually sold without designer sub-branding, and instead used internal or external design teams capable of responding to any whiff of change in market trends. ▶▶

### SONY D50

Alongside the Walkman's success, the compact disc was also developing rapidly. And while the Walkman had not been any great technological leap forward, the first personal CD was at the time an astonishing feat of miniaturization. It was made possible only by large-scale integration of the digital circuitry and reductions in the size and power consumption of the scanning laser and disc-drive mechanism. Even so, Sony's first Discman personal CD player looks decidedly clunky to twenty-first-century eyes. It also used up batteries relatively quickly and had poor shock resistance though this would soon improve as "anti-jogging" memory systems developed.

▶

date of introduction: **1985, Japan**

size: **13 x 12.5 x 4 cm (5¼ x 5 x 1¾ in)**

key features: **early personal CD player; rechargeable batteries**

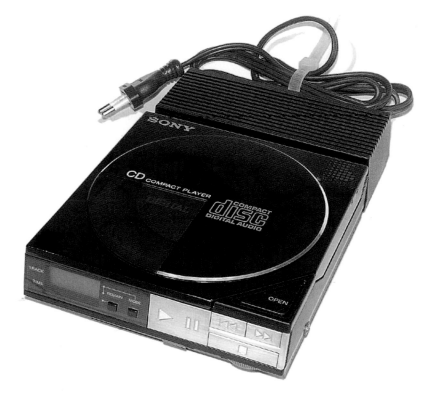

## PHILIPS ROLLER

Portable audio styling was becoming more diverse. Philips' Roller and Moving Sound series marked a shift away from plain surfaces and rectangular shapes. They also showed a global company segmenting a global market by age and lifestyle rather than by national tastes. Begun as a student project by British designer Graham Hinde, the Roller was taken up by Philips, which had recently set up a "youth task force" in an attempt to throw off its traditional image. The casual graphics and "roller-skates" speaker detailing, as well as the use of colour, were part of an integrated design concept that extended across all the packaging and publicity material for the product.

One of the most influential of these design teams was frogdesign. From small beginnings working for Wega in Germany, it became an international design group with major clients such as Apple and Sony. It played a big part in creating a new language for product design in the 1980s, taking German functionalism traditionally associated with names like Braun, and softening it with user-friendly contoured shapes, colour, and whimsical styling details. For the ripples of postmodernism and the Memphis "anti-design" group were spreading into the high street. Memphis – a short-lived early '80s reaction to the monotonous good taste of much '70s furniture and product design – was the brainchild of the designer and architect Ettore Sottsass, and it had the same kind of invigorating effect on some young designers as punk had had on music and fashion a few years earlier.

Portable audio styles in particular became more diverse, with Sharp's radio recorders (see right) and Toshiba's personal stereos dressed in '50s pastel shades or strong primary colours, and Philips' Roller (see left) and Moving Sound series marking an early shift away from plain surfaces and rectangular shapes. Black might still dominate the audio market, but with functionality taken for granted, equipment no longer needed to look technical; and a focus on surfaces and a little playfulness in colour, shape, and typography were in order.

▼

date of introduction: **1986, Netherlands**

size: **44 x 21 x 12 cm (17¼ x 8¼ x 4¾ in)**

key features: **use of colour and distinctive styling**

## CONCRETE STEREO

While the new design museums displayed mass-produced consumer products like works of art, Ron Arad's jagged-edged Concrete Stereo actually was a limited-edition artwork as much as a functional object. Most of Arad's designs were made individually, often re-using existing objects, like the Rover chair, which he made from a leather car seat. Here the reinforced concrete offers a surreal contrast to the precisely made arm and platter.

## SHARP QT50

Sharp's radio recorders came in '50s pastel shades of pink, green, or ivory, as well as primary colours. The "retro" style might induce nostalgia in some, but in the postmodern '80s it was just one "look" plucked from a diversity of choices, without any connection being made to the past.

▲

date of introduction: **1984, UK**

designer: **Ron Arad**

size: **50 x 40 x 8cm (19³/₄ x 15³/₄ x 3¹/₄in)**

key feature: **limited edition intervention into audio design**

▼

date of introduction: **1984, Japan**

size: **40 x 14 x 8 cm (15³/₄ x 5¹/₂ x 3¹/₄in)**

key feature: **use of "retro" colour and shape**

▲ After specializing in valve amplifiers
during the '80s, Audio Innovations in
Britain developed the Alto range of solid-
state separates with what one reviewer
called "post-retro bodywork".

# 1990- a **converging** world

The last years of the twentieth century saw audio linking with TV, video, and computer equipment to provide an increasingly seamless world of information and entertainment.

## More silver – and gold – discs

Recent years have seen a diverse range of entertainment electronics, with a range of possibilities. These are mostly based around the familiar twelve-centimetre (four-and-three-quarter-inch) CD format – for playing and recording digital signals, whether audio, video, or other content.

The '90s saw CD become the dominant music carrier, with sales over-taking those of pre-recorded cassettes early in the decade. Personal CD players were now commonplace, while the CD was at the heart of small and stylish lifestyle systems for the home. There was also greater accept-ance of CD by audiophiles. This was partly pragmatic – most music could not be bought any other way – but was also due to better player technology.

The start of the millennium brought much publicity from the record and hardware industries about new audio disc formats. Here the audio story becomes inextricably linked with video and the Digital Versatile Disc (DVD) – one of the fastest-growing products in consumer electronics.

From 1990 the basic CD was followed by formats offering combin-ations of text, images, interactive data, and, eventually, full-motion video. Many of these failed to get a hold on the market, though CD-ROMs became established as high-capacity carriers for computer data, allowing computer owners to play CDs that could also carry artist-related software. ▶▶

## WADIA 270 CD TRANSPORT

Wadia was founded in 1988. This 24kg (53lb) unit contains only the "transport" for the compact disc: it is teamed with a separate digital/ analogue "decoding computer" that feeds an amplifier. Over 13.5kg (30lb) of machined aluminium chassis components help to isolate critical parts mechanically, while state-of-the-art fibre-optic technology is used for signal connections. The styling is in the minimalist black-box tradition. In no-compromise audio, the law of diminishing returns applies; for the personal CD player opposite performs essentially the same functions in one pocket-sized case.

▶

date of introduction: **1998, US**

size: **18 x 43 x 42 cm (7 x 17 x 16½ in)**

key features: **CD transport; heavyweight construction**

## TECHNICS PERSONAL CD

Compared with the first CD personal players (see p.123), this Technics model from the '90s is wafer-thin and little wider than the diameter of the disc dictates. By now CD personal players often had a curved, clam-like structure with the lid integrated into the overall design of the body, while improvements in plastics gave a high-quality, almost metallic feel. High-capacity memory chips had fallen in price since the '80s and could now store about a minute's worth of music in digital form; this meant that if the player was jogged, the back-up memory could continue to stream the sound while the laser got back on track.

▼

date of introduction: **1991, Japan**

size: **15 x 13 x 2 cm (6 x 5 x ¾ in)**

key features: **slim design; integrated shape**

▲ By the '90s boom boxes had a softer, more sculptured shape and often had CD as well as cassette and radio.

▲

date of introduction: **1998, Japan**

size: **45 x 30.5 x 10 cm (17¾ x 12 x 4 in)**

key features: **"lifestyle" aesthetic; top-loading CD player**

## MARANTZ LAYLA

In the late '90s designers broke away from the black-box shape into a variety of new presentations for CD/radio combinations, which were promoted as "lifestyle audio". In the process, the top-loading format returned to prominence. Gracefully opening glass doors or the CD visibly spinning behind a glass panel gave a touch of sci-fi magic and some of the visual involvement with the medium that had been lost with the abandonment of vinyl. On the Layla, the CD player and radio are concealed under a lid which lifts at the touch of a button. When the lid is closed four joysticks control the main functions.

By the early '90s recordable CD technology had been developed. At first this was an expensive "write-once" process – the disc could not be erased and reused – but 1995 saw the first home CD-R decks from Pioneer (see opposite). By the end of the decade CD-R drives for home computers had made it cheap and simple with the right software to "rip" tracks from commercial CDs and "burn" new compilation discs. At the same time, audio companies produced CD recorders and systems using either CD-R or rewritable (CD-RW) discs, which could be used again and again. Making an identical copy of a CD was just a matter of pressing a button.

### Video enters the picture

Since the early '80s, large "laserdiscs" had been a potential replacement for video cassettes, but, since they could not record, take-up was limited. Attempts to extend the CD format to video were also beset by problems. But, by the mid '90s, DVDs were offering high-quality video and (with the right equipment) the surround-sound experience of the cinema, plus extra content (such as subtitles or out-takes), all in a familiar format, which meant DVD players would play audio CDs too. Crucially, DVDs were backed by the movie industry, and, as a further sign of how different media were converging, Sony PlayStation 2 game consoles could also play DVDs.

While sound quality had previously been a low priority for most TV buyers, the coming of stereo sound and then the concept of home cinema (or home theatre) raised its status and hastened the merging of audio and video equipment in people's living rooms. First, Dolby ▶▶

## TAG McLAREN APHRODITE

TAG McLaren is best known for its Formula 1 motor-racing team and TAG Heuer watches. Whether the company's Aphrodite audio system is an example of technology transfer from advanced F1 car electronics, or a smart marketing exercise, it is certainly a provocative piece of styling, targeting a younger demographic than, for example, Bang & Olufsen. Like the Marantz Layla opposite, it marks a trend towards sci-fi "loading bays" for CDs. Design details such as the solid-metal CD clamp also show the way CD players now seek the visual and tactile appeal of vinyl turntables. It comes in eight colours, reminiscent of '50s personalization.

▼

date of introduction: **1999, UK**

size: **50 x 12 x 33 cm (19¾ x 4¾ x 13 in)**

key features: **single-bit CD player; RDS radio tuner; eight colours**

▲ The Pioneer PDR-05 was the first deck aimed at consumers (rather than at professionals) to use the recordable CD-R format. In 1995 it cost £1300 or $2000.

Aphrodite
AvantGarde

"Style a-plenty and performance to match; no other system looks like the Aphrodite or is built to these high standards"
★★★★★
What Hi-fi? - September 2000

"Nobody would expect such completeness, superiority and dynamic scale from such a compact system. Aphrodite demonstrated multi-layered sound ability and resolved the finest details of the music... The loudspeaker Calliope is a sensitive partner, transparent, homogeneous and dynamically convincing. They are a perfect fit."

AUDIO - May 2000

*Aphrodite is available in eight metallic colours, shown here in royal blue with Calliope loudspeakers, in silver.*

www.tagmclarenaudio.com

## SONY MZR91

Not much bigger than the Minidisc itself, when it was launched this Sony personal MD Walkman was the smallest recording model in the world, yet it allowed up to twenty-nine hours of recording time. Using the jog lever at the side and the slim remote controller with back-lit liquid crystal display in the headphone lead, users can compile their choice of music via a digital optical connection and move, label, combine, or delete individual tracks at will. For prestige personal audio products like this, the precision feel and jewel-like finish of a metal housing is vital; the MZR91 has a blue aluminium top cover while the MZR90 variant is housed in silver-coloured magnesium alloy.

▶

date of introduction: **1999, Japan**

size: **9 x 9 x 1cm (3½ x 3½ x ½in)**

key features: **smallest recording Minidisc; in-line remote control**

surround-sound added a rear and then a centre-front "dialogue" channel to normal stereo, while digital systems increased the number of channels to five or more (plus an extra bass channel). Multi-channel hi-fi amplifiers or receivers were available, but audio systems that included DVD and the extra speakers with the usual stereo package also became big sellers. In fact the success of DVD led to a debate over the merits of surround-sound that in many ways echoed the "stereo versus mono" debate of the '50s.

The next step is recordable DVD, which can store video, music, or other content on a blank disc, though it is proving hard to agree on a format. At the time of writing, Blu-ray – which uses a new kind of blue laser – is attracting wide industry support. Other companies have explored the possibility of recording TV or audio on a computer-like hard disk.

### Other digital developments

Because CD-R developed first as a computer peripheral, the record industry failed to stop it being used as a home audio medium until too late. Things were different with digital tape. Direct digital copying (from a CD, for instance) is a sensitive issue because (unlike old-style analogue tape) there is no loss of quality however many times each copy is recopied. The launch and promotion of mass-market digital recording was held up by insistence on "copy management" systems to prevent mass copying. A case in point was DAT (see p.110), which, though adopted by music professionals, hardly penetrated the consumer market in most countries. ▶▶

## KENWOOD HM-DV7

A good example of current trends in media convergence, this Kenwood system plays DVDs, CDs, and recordable CDs (including MP3 music files), and has an AM/FM tuner. It has a sub-woofer (on the left) plus a single surround-sound speaker. The light metal and use of colour reflects the twenty-first-century aesthetic.

## MUSICAL FIDELITY X-RAY

This CD player has a sophisticated twenty-four-bit digital-to-analogue converter (DAC) to give a detailed and transparent sound very close to the theoretical limit of the sixteen-bit CD format. But the rounded cross section gives the unit a slightly retro feel – quite different from Musical Fidelity's minimalist A1 (see p.115).

▲

date of introduction: **2001, Japan**

size: **14 x 14 x 36 cm (5½ x 5½ x 14¼ in)**

key features: **multimedia home system with virtual surround-sound**

▼

date of introduction: **1995, UK**

size: **23 x 11 x 35 cm (9 x 4¼ x 13¾ in)**

key features: **high-end CD player; twenty-four-bit DAC converter**

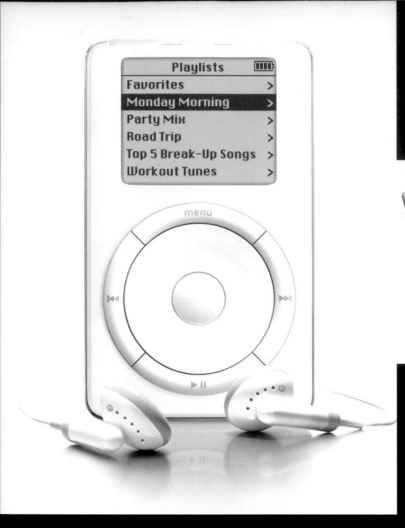

◄ ▲ The Apple iPod MP3 player can store up to a thousand tracks on its hard drive. The itunes software makes it easy to download songs and playlists from a Mac computer.

# ok computers

Listening to music at home is very different from sharing it in a club, but '90s dance styles had a continuing effect on the music people bought for themselves.

The principle of making music in a studio, which can then be heard at home, was no longer sacrosanct. Since the '50s music recording has seen a huge shift: from capturing authentic "live" performances to being an integral part of a mass electronic culture in which multi-layered sound mixes – part digital composition,

The CD was followed by a series of developments extending its capability to store video and data as well as audio. And, by the late '90s, widespread computer ownership was putting new power in the hands of consumers. Music might increasingly be owned and controlled by big corporations, but file-sharing networks like the pioneering Napster site posed a massive challenge to their power. Home computers also made it easier than ever to rip tracks from CDs

PROPELLERHEADS
DECKSANDDRUMSANDROCKANDROLL

▲ Trance DJ Sasha in action at the 2001 Homelands dance festival in Hampshire, UK.

◄ The Propellerheads' 1998 release *Decksanddrumsandrockandroll* blended breakbeat techno, hip-hop, and recycled '60s film music, the title summing up the "anything goes" attitude to musical genres at the turn of the millennium.

▲

date of introduction: **1995, UK**

designer: **Conrad Mas**

size: **18 x 41 x 40 cm (7 x 16¼ x 15¾in)**

key feature: **anti-vibration record clamp and suspension system**

## AVID ACUTUS

Avid's stated aim was to "take vinyl into the twenty-first century". Like other high-end turntables, the Acutus has a belt-drive and a sprung sub-chassis, while the polymer platter mat and screw-down record clamp aim to limit unwanted stylus vibrations which might otherwise spoil sound quality. The cylindrical pillars not only give the Acutus its striking appearance but have suspension springs to isolate it from external vibration. An outboard power supply (not shown) feeds the motor, driving a massive 10kg (22lb) platter with sapphire bearing.

Around 1992 two digital formats were promoted as a replacement for ordinary cassettes: Digital Compact Cassette (DCC), developed by Philips, never got enough backing from other companies to catch on, but Sony's Minidisc was more elegant, being a 6.5mm (2½in) laser/magnetic disc in a slim plastic caddy rather like a computer disk. Using powerful electronic compression of the digital data (removing virtually inaudible parts of the music signal), it was convenient (tracks could easily be accessed, edited, and organized) and was widely adopted as a record/playback medium in tiny personal portables as well as home systems.

Meanwhile, as CD sales levelled off, record companies were keen to establish a new premium-priced music format. In 1999 DVD-Audio was trailed as a new audio format with higher quality and multi-channel capabilities, but the launch was delayed by debate over anti-copying. Sony and Philips were the driving force behind an alternative, Super Audio CD, which also has surround-sound as a selling point. But, with CD well-established and the possibility that music purchase may become a virtual business, downloaded from a broadband link or the Internet, it is not clear how commercially sustainable these new formats will be.

◄

date of introduction: **1995, Italy**

size: **32 x 22 x 12 cm (12½ x 9 x 4¾ in)**

key features: **compact twin-mono integrated amplifer; fashion colours**

## Hi-fi blossoms again

With the big players now more interested in growth areas such as DVD and personal audio, the '90s saw a blossoming of smaller hi-fi manufacturers, though many also got involved in multi-channel sound in some way. Some companies emerged from periods of financial difficulty with renewed stability, such as Quad, which, after big losses in the early 1990s, is now owned by a group committed to its traditions and the introduction of new valve equipment. Another was Marantz, which relaunched some of its classic equipment from the '60s during the decade. ▶▶

### SYNTHESIS NIMIS

Synthesis – under the slogan '"art in music" – is one of several Italian companies (see also Unison Research, p.7) that produce tube amplifiers with a very high standard of finish. At first available in wood, black, and chrome, the Nimis now sports a range of i-Mac style colours with white detailing. Essentially a simple design, and small by the standards of most similar products, the Nimis is an integrated amplifier only just over 30cm (12in) wide. The metal cage protects the hand from the hot tubes when operating the volume or input selection controls at the front.

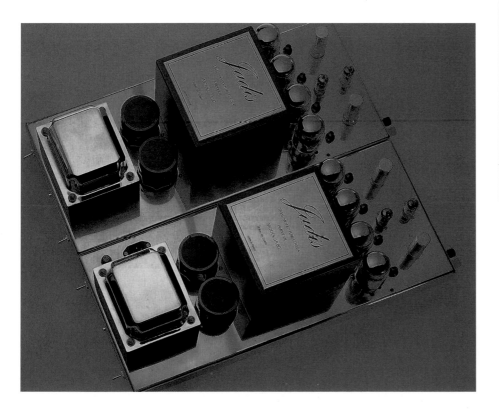

◄ These large twin monoblock JA80 power amplifiers are from the French company Jadis.

## ORACLE CD2000

This is probably about as far as any company has gone in appropriating the aesthetic of the vinyl turntable for a CD player. Oracle claims that vibration of the rapidly spinning CD can affect the accuracy of the scanning laser and stretch the capacity of error-correction circuits, with harmful effects on sound. A magnetic clamp and flexible plastic washer help prevent this "disc chatter", while the whole player is isolated from external vibration by a suspension system of springs and dampers inherited from vinyl turntables such as the Delphi (see p.115). Construction is almost entirely of solid aluminium.

Despite the virtual disappearance of LPs from the mass market, vinyl was by no means dead. Apart from its place on the dance scene, classic albums were issued in new high-quality pressings, often costing more than a CD, for the home market. With vinyl mainly the province of enthusiasts and small suppliers, there was a growing interest in craft-built turntables and arms valued for their visual style and eclectic use of materials as well as their sound quality. Vintage turntables were snapped up by keen collectors or were lovingly restored by specialist companies dedicated to keeping famous marques alive. Especially in the US, Japan, Germany, and Italy, there was a passion for the exclusiveness of aesthetically distinctive amplifiers, produced in small numbers.

### The high-end aesthetic

A vintage turntable or amplifier is visually satisfying because of its authenticity and solid, utilitarian lines. New high-end products may strive for a similar aesthetic and are often massively over-engineered as a result (by contrast, a cheap CD personal player is manufactured with microscopic precision, but gives few visual clues that this is so). Other high-end hi-fi may be more stylized in its use of colour, form, or materials, but will still offer the allure of the unusual, the non-standard, or the personalized.

At this level audio equipment may become an "installation" in the artistic as well as technical sense. Use of such equipment, with its consciously archaic technology and lack of automation, involves elements ▶▶

▲

date of introduction: **1998, Canada**

size: **42.5 x 36 x 15 cm (16¾ x 14 x 6 in)**

key features: **record-like clamp and suspension system**

## SPJ LA LUCE CS CENTOVENTI

Few women designers have been identifiably associated with audio design. An exception is Dutch designer Judy Spotheim-Koreneef, whose La Luce turntable takes the idea of hi-fi as sculpture to extremes. The name is appropriate given the design's extensive use of light-transmitting acrylic. Despite its massiveness (the platter, machined from a solid acrylic block weighted around the rim, is 12 cm (4¾in) thick and weighs 18 kg (40 lb), there is a visual lightness to the structure, which is enhanced by the stainless-steel motor linked by a delicate belt. The German Clearaudio designs (see back cover) are among the few others to match La Luce's visual presence.

▲

date of introduction: **2000, Netherlands**

designer: **Judy Spotheim-Koreneef**

size: **42 x 34 x 29 cm (16½ x 13½ x 11½ in)**

key features: **use of acrylic**

▼ A US design which has steadily developed over more than ten years, the VPI TNT features an acrylic platform on a four-point compressed-air suspension, and a laminated platter of aluminium and lead-filled acrylic.

date of introduction: **1991, Germany**

size: **95 x 83 x 162 cm
(37¼ x 32¾ x 63¾ in)**

key features: **moulded horns; striking
appearance**

▶

date of introduction: **2000, UK**

size: **34 x 21 x 22 cm (13¼ x 8¼ x 8¾ in)**

key features: **injection-moulded cabinet;
irregular shape**

## AVANTGARDE TRIO

Described as a homage to horn
pioneers Paul Klipsch and Paul Voigt,
the Trio's three horns (for upper bass,
middle, and treble) are made of ABS
plastic mounted on a metal frame. A
separate subwoofer (not visible)
provides deep bass. The Trio Classico
variant is shown on the front cover.

## BLUEROOM MINIPOD

A spin-off from the B&W company, the
Minipod's endearingly organic shape
has the acoustic advantage of
reducing resonances and reflections.
It stands on tripod legs or hangs on
the wall, and the transparent blue and
grey finish – like so many late 1990s
products – shows the influence of the
Apple i-Mac.

of ritual and expertise, and visual and tactile links with how the music is actually reproduced. These factors, taken for granted by hi-fi enthusiasts in the '50s, perhaps give new satisfaction in an era when most equipment is reduced to an assembly of microchips and invisible motors.

## Loudspeakers all around

The renewed interest in older and often larger types of loudspeaker gave designers free rein with cabinet styles. Examples on these pages include the brashly extrovert Avantgarde horn models from Germany (left) or the sculptural B&W Nautilus and Carfrae Little Big Horn (see p.142).

At the other extreme, the growth of surround-sound encouraged speakers to be inconspicuous, or at least space-saving. It became popular to hand the bass reproduction over to a sub-woofer tucked away out of full view, allowing the "satellite" speakers to be small and stylish. Such speakers were often housed in aluminium pods instead of wooden boxes.

Another development that may radically change the look of speakers is the NXT flat panel. Most speakers need some kind of enclosure to control the sound waves, but NXT's technology uses a small "exciter" attached to a flat panel which makes it vibrate. The system has been licensed to many other manufacturers and its flatness lends itself to for use elsewhere, for example in speakers in car-doors or computer screens. German companies have been the most innovative early users, with see-through speaker panels (see p.2) and picture-frame designs to be hung on the wall. ▶▶

### O'HEOCHA D2·ISO·5

Aonghus O'hEocha is an automotive design engineer and the company's range is typical of a current trend towards pod-like speakers having aesthetic links with classic car fitments, while also – on their sputnik-style spikes or long single-stalk floorstands – often having an androidal look. On this model, the high frequency tweeter is mounted in a solid aluminium housing at the top, while two mid-range units occupy the centre spherical section of aluminium alloy damped with a composite material. Two reflexed bass drivers in the base section complete the system.

◀

date of introduction: **2001, Ireland**

designer: **Aonghus O'hEocha**

size: **94 x 37 cm diameter (37 x 14⅛ in)**

key features: **three-section design; metal enclosure**

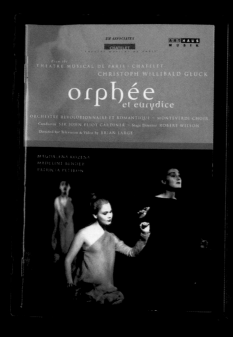

◄ DVD is an ideal format for opera recordings, providing high-quality pictures and sound, as well as the option of subtitles.

## lifestyle

The '90s saw a sea-change in home entertainment. As home cinema arrived, the old boundaries between the TV and the stereo began to break down. By the end of the decade widescreen TVs, digital satellite channels, and DVD players were offering huge pictures with six channels of window-rattling surround-sound. Meanwhile the "lifestyle" aesthetic became more important than ever, with elegant components blending neatly into the décor and "interconnectivity" promising all the digital systems would work flawlessly together.

This merging of media was mirrored in the way that media and entertainment companies merged and expanded. By 2000 music had become part of a global consumer machine, with 90 per cent of all CDs in the West distributed by just five companies. And Sony – a company playing a major part in any audio

history – now not only sells TVs and stereo equipment but also owns a major record label, film production company, and the market-leading PlayStation game system. Such a reach gives Sony huge opportunities for inter-related marketing, for weaving its brand into every aspect of our lives. Meanwhile new formats like SA-CD or DVD-Audio may give the record companies the chance to remarket their back catalogue.

With any kind of content transmittable or storable as a digital data stream, the future may lie in virtual networks and software rather than in turntables, tapes, and transistors. The music business has always feared new technologies, which seem to undermine its power. In the end it could probably make more money by selling downloadable data than pieces of plastic and metal. But would the buying public be happy with that?

▲ Multiple speaker systems (like these from KEF) are now part of the home cinema experience.

◄ Home computers can be used to download music and video of singers like Kylie Minogue.

## Radio – the future?

In Europe RDS technology allowed FM station names to be displayed and automatic retuning and access to traffic newsflashes. RDS became widespread on in-car audio and spread to home equipment in the '90s.

Digital audio broadcasting was developed by an international group of broadcasters and manufacturers, though the US seems likely to go for a different system for digital radio. DAB provides better in-car reception, and spectrum space for many more channels as well as data – such as song lyrics – to be transmitted. Existing FM stations have been joined by new digital-only channels. But digital receivers have proved expensive and impracticable for portable use, though the Psion Wavefinder (see p.149) offers a stylish and totally new radio aesthetic, and cable or satellite TV services often include radio channels as part of the package.

Meanwhile AM and FM broadcasting – especially long-distance short-wave radio – faces competition from the Internet, through which thousands of radio stations throughout the world can be accessed. ▶▶

### BEOSYSTEM 2500

Jakob Jensen's iconic '70s designs for Bang & Olufsen had transferred less successfully to the matt-black '80s and tough competition obliged the company to form an alliance with Philips. By the early 1990s, however, a new design director, David Lewis (who had been Jensen's assistant) was bringing a new freshness to the brand. His striking vertical Beosystem 2500 was among the first to place the spinning CD on open display. The glass doors that glide open as a hand approaches provide a pleasing element of ritual. The use of colour and glass as strong elements of styling was influential during the decade.

▲

date of introduction: **2000, Japan**

size: **125 x 25 x 25 cm (49¼ x 9¾ x 9¾ in)**

key features: **surround-sound system;
adaptable unit positioning**

◄

date of introduction: **1991, Denmark**

designer: **David Lewis**

size: **32 x 36 x 16 cm (12½ x 14 ¼ x 6¼ in)**

key features: **CD visible while playing;
early use of colour and glass**

## NAKAMICHI SOUNDSPACE 11

The Nakamichi SoundSpace 11 is
typical of current preoccupations with
home cinema and lifestyle flexibility. It
has a five-disc DVD/CD changer with
touch-panel controls, Dolby Digital
and DTS surround-sound processor,
five-channel speaker system (front
and rear left and right, plus front
centre) with two sub-woofers. The
units can be arranged in a variety of
ways: on shelves, on walls, or on
floor pedestals, while "multi-zoning"
means a movie may be watched in
one room while an FM broadcast is
listened to in another.

## MP3 shakes the record industry

In the personal sector, cassette players were increasingly replaced by CD and, later in the decade, Minidisc players, many of which would record as well. Players became slimmer and lighter, often adopting a shape similar to the medium itself: round for CD, square for Minidisc.

In 1999 the personal player line-up was joined by the MP3 player. MP3 is a software application for digitally compressing music. MP3 files can be sent or received over the Internet reasonably quickly, and burned onto a recordable CD, or stored on the memory chip of a tiny solid-state portable player such as the Rio (see p.150). MP3 soon became a convenient shorthand for the concept, but in fact some companies used different compression software that limited recording of copyright material. Some MP3 players also use a small magnetic storage disc with a higher capacity, or offer sophisticated "jukebox" facilities for programming tracks.

MP3 and similar players are now being combined with other personal products such as mobile phones, cameras, and personal organizers. An interesting design aspect of computer-based audio is how the actual hardware's three-dimensional curves, push-buttons, and slider controls are meticulously recreated on screen to provide graphic visual appeal.

File-sharing or "peer-to-peer" websites – of which Napster was the first to become famous – allow users to search for tracks on another user's computer and download them free of charge, as well as to post their own tracks for others to access. Napster quickly became hugely popular – at least with the young and computer-literate – with millions of music ▶▶

### ALESSI POE

The Poe radio is in interesting contrast to the Lexon Tykho opposite as, while targeting similar markets, its pull on the consumer is based almost entirely on branding: the status of both its designer (Philippe Starck) and its manufacturer (Alessi). Starck (b.1949) worked on furniture and interior design but became a celebrity beyond the design world in the 1990s through his instantly recognizable and assiduously promoted household objects, which include lights, toothbrushes, and kitchen accessories.

▶

date of introduction: **1997, Italy**

designer: **Philippe Starck**

size: **24.5 x 18 x 16.5cm (9¾ x 7 x 6¾in)**

key features: **painted polystyrene body; use of branding**

## PSION WAVEFINDER

Many digital (DAB) radios have been ungainly or bulky, but Psion's eye-catching Wavefinder is neither. Essentially an antenna nearly 70cm (27½in) long, it plugs into the USB port of a personal computer. Pulsating coloured lights in the centre section, which contains the electronics, add to the space-age effect. Its software searches for stations or download-able games and displays them on screen, while audio can be recorded as an MP3 file.

## LEXON TYKHO

The '90s saw an explosion of "designer" objects targeted at endlessly sub-dividing markets and the lifestyle media. Lexon's products – watches, pens, radios, travel items – successfully tapped into this trend for desirable personal accessories. Thus Marc Berthier's rubber radio may be just a radio, but it is one that featured on the cover of *Time*, under the headline "'The Rebirth of Design".

▲

date of introduction: **2000, UK**

size: **68 x 8 x 7 cm (26¾ x 3¼ x 2¾in)**

key features: **low-cost digital radio; links with computer**

▼

date of introduction: **1997, France**

designer: **Marc Berthier**

size: **14 x 8 x 4 cm (5½ x 3¼ x 1½in)**

key features: **rubber case; combined twist tuning/antenna**

files downloaded every day. Seeing its cash flow threatened, the music industry took legal action, forcing Napster to close, and setting up similar, but paid-for services such as MusicNet and Pressplay. But so far these have not proved popular, while other free file-swapping applications, like Gnutella and Morpheus, are proving tougher to control because, (unlike Napster), they are totally decentralized and network-based.

The question is: will consumers be content to buy music in a totally virtual interaction? Some argue that many will always want to own a "trophy", a tangible example of the work of their favourite artists, and will still see shopping for music as a pleasurable leisure activity.

## The CAD/CAM revolution

Recent styling idioms have been linked to the growth of computer-aided design (CAD), which revolutionized product development in the '80s and '90s. Though the principles of CAD had been developed at the Massachusetts Institute of Technology in the 1950s, many years passed before computers were cheap and powerful enough for general use by product designers. But now, instead of the time-consuming drawing and model-making of previous decades, a product designer can fairly quickly prepare drawings and three-dimensional full-colour models on-screen for a range of possible design options. These can easily be rotated, altered in size or colour, or manipulated to produce cross-sectional views. But this is not the end of the story: computer-aided manufacture (CAM) software can use the CAD data to control the automated cutting tools or robots (possibly thousands of miles away) in the actual production process.

Because the time from initial concept to working prototype is shorter, companies can launch new products more quickly, or produce small-batch variants for different markets. Most significantly, CAD/CAM has made it easier and cheaper to design and manufacture products with complex ▶▶

### RIO 300

MP3 is a software application for digitally compressing music, so it can be sent over the Internet, burned on to a CD, or stored on the memory chip of a tiny solid-state player. Rio – at first called Diamond Rio – was one of the prime movers in this last market. While most MP3 players use "flash memory" chips (whose size limits how much music can be stored and at what quality), others use a small magnetic storage disk with a higher capacity, while Sony's Network Walkman uses a "Memory Stick"– a removable digital storage device about the size of a piece of chewing gum. Like many current personal products, the Rio is shaped to fit the hand.

▶

date of introduction: **2001, Germany**

size: **18 x 5cm (7 x 2 in)**

key features: **digital radio; MP3 playback**

◀

date of introduction: **1998, US**

size: **9 x 6.5 x 2 cm (3⅛ x 2½ x ¾ in)**

key features: **early MP3 player; sculptured hand-held shape; flash memory storage**

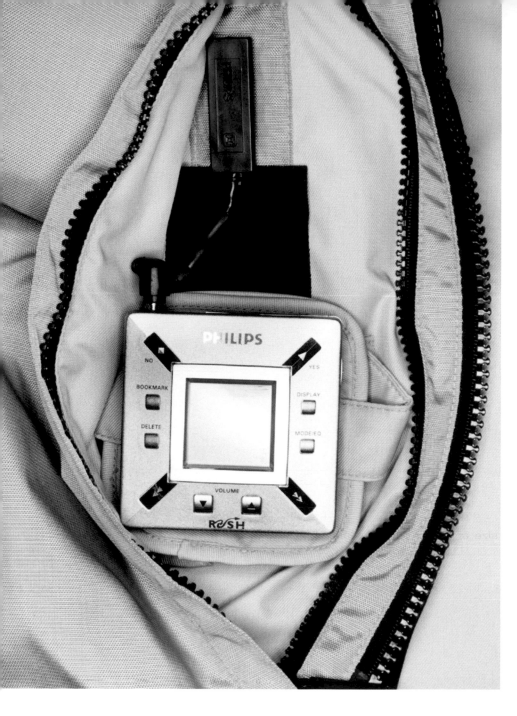

◄ In the 1990s the mobile phone hugely reinforced the popularity (which began with the Walkman) of fashionable technology worn on the person. The Philips Rush took this concept a stage further with personal technology (in this case an MP3 player) integrated into customized clothing.

## BLAUPUNKT WOODSTOCK

Blaupunkt (the name means "Blue Spot") produced its first car radio in 1932 and became a brand synonymous with car audio, with developments in stereo, CD, driving navigation aids, and anti-theft security devices. Blaupunkt models are often named after gritty urban centres, for example Berlin, Amsterdam, or New York. In contrast, the Woodstock has a rustic '60s aura, but it is bang up to date, combining digital RDS radio, CD, and MP3 player in a standard-sized enclosure. MP3s can be played from CD-ROM or multi-media cards compatible with mobile phones, while the panel design shows the typical use of menu-driven touch controls and alphanumeric displays.

curves, and this has had a far-reaching effect on design, while a car or a radio-recorder from the 1980s now looks remarkably boxy and angular, both now have much more refined, sculptural forms.

## Sound design for a better lifestyle

As the technology gap between leading companies gets smaller, and technology itself shrinks, the design of equipment is more important than ever. Hi-fi seems to remain a mainly male preoccupation, and the latest high-tech gadgets are still often seen by the media as '"toys for boys". But, like cars, audio products are now being marketed in a more sophisticated way to both women and men; they are presented as routes to self-expression and individual creativity. The past decade has seen multinational companies, in particular, adopting ever more sweeping strategies to involve consumers in an emotional attachment to their brand. For whether a transistor radio, a hi-fi system, or the latest MP3 player, sound designs have always been more than mere bundles of electronics: designers and manufacturers hope to tap into consumers' aspirations and make their products part of people's lifestyles. As a Sony advertisement claims, it is "A company devoted to the celebration of life... we are not here to be logical. Or predictable. We are here to pursue infinite possibilities... we help dreamers dream."

### AIWA XSG5

This relatively discreet "style system" shows the typically twenty-first century use of silver, light wood finishes, and pale fabrics. The profile of the front panel is softly contoured. A motorized panel slides upwards to reveal the three-disc CD compartment. Such small touches of luxury and automation add to user satisfaction and the perceived value of the product. A "sleep" timer points to the fact that such systems are no longer confined to the living room. It has remote control, which has become a standard feature of audio systems like this one.

▶

date of introduction: **2001**

size: **26 x 27 x 36 cm (10¼ x 10½ x 14¼ in) (main unit)**

key features: **three-CD changer; cassette and radio**

## JVC MX-GT91R

By contrast with the Aiwa system (left), this JVC system for the "youth market" throws together an extraordinary mix of styling motifs from Harley Davidson to Richard Rogers – like the Pompidou Centre, it seems to wear its technology on the outside. But while its "advanced labyrinth aero port system sub-woofer" may raise a smile, such techno-hype is nothing new in sound design.

## NOKIA 5510

The mobile phone has become an even more powerful symbol of personal identity than the Walkman. Nokia's 5510 links a phone with a stereo FM radio and digital recorder/player which can copy CDs or download music files. The styling, with its central display and split keyboard, is a fusion of games console and mobile.

▲
date of introduction: **2001**

size: **37 x 33.5 x 26.5 cm (14½ x 13¼ x 10⅝ in)**

key features: **CD/radio/cassette system; six speakers; dance club, hall, and stadium effects**

▼
date of introduction: **2001, Finland**

size: **13.5 x 6 x 3 cm (5⅓ x 2⅓ x 1¼ in)**

key features: **WAP phone; digital recorder; FM radio**

# glossary

**Active loudspeaker**  a loudspeaker incorporating its own specially designed power amplification

**Analogue**  usually refers to a system where sound waves are directly represented by variations in something else – most obviously a record groove; but also an electrical signal in an amplifier or magnetic patterns on a tape. On a radio with analogue tuning, station frequency is indicated by a pointer moving along a scale. (See **Digital**)

**Baffle**  the panel on which a loudspeaker drive unit is mounted

**Bass-reflex**  speaker cabinet design with a port to reinforce bass reproduction

**Binaural**  the sound given by "stereo" headphones, where (unlike loudspeakers) each ear hears only the left or right channel from the equipment

**Cartridge**  the unit fitted into the end of a tone-arm, carrying the stylus which tracks the record groove. Reversing the loudspeaker principle, it turns stylus vibrations into an electrical signal. Can also mean a packaged tape system, as in eight-track cartridge

**CD-R/CD-RW**  compact disc format that allows recording. Rewritable (RW) discs and systems allow erasure and re-recording

**Channel**  most often, the left and right signal paths of a stereo amplifier. Or, in surround-sound (or multi-channel) systems, one of up to five or more

**Control unit**  see **Pre-amplifier**

**Crossover**  in a loudspeaker, components that feed the different parts of the frequency spectrum to the appropriate drive unit

**DAB**  Digital Audio Broadcasting – see p.146

**DAC**  Digital-to-analogue converter, either built into a CD player, or available as a separate unit

**Digital**  any system where a sound wave or other analogue signal is electronically sampled (measured) tens of thousands of times a second and the result represented as a stream of bits (digital data) which can, for example, be stored as a spiral of microscopically small pits on a CD, or sent over the Internet. On a digital radio, the frequency of the wanted station is synthesized by the circuitry and displayed as a number rather than on an analogue tuning scale

**Distortion**  any unwanted change to a signal passing through a system, for example causing a roughening of the sound that is uncomfortable to listen to. There are many causes, but examples include cartridge tracking error or amplifier overloading

**Dolby**  one of several noise reduction or surround-sound systems (see Index)

**Drive unit**  one of the bass, mid-frequency, or treble units mounted in a loudspeaker cabinet

**DVD-Audio**  audio development of DVD video discs offering multi-channel sound and better quality than ordinary CDs

**Dynamic range**  the range between the quietest and loudest sounds that a system can accurately reproduce. They are usually limited by background noise and overload distortion respectively

**Electrostatic**  usually refers to a loudspeaker in which sound is produced by an electrically charged membrane stretched between metal grids fed from the amplifier

**Equalization**  process where frequencies are boosted or cut on a tape or disc, and corrected by the playing equipment to produce a flat frequency response

**Feedback**  sound from loudspeakers, for example, may "feed back" to a turntable and spoil reproduction. "Negative feedback" is an amplifier circuit technique that cancels out distortion to some extent

**Filter**  correction circuit on, for example, an amplifier to reduce noise

**Frequency response**  ideally, a system should reproduce equally the whole sound spectrum from low bass to high treble frequencies – this is called a flat frequency response. Technical specifications should show how closely equipment meets this ideal

**Gain**  the amount by which a signal is amplified in a piece of equipment

**High-end**  term for expensive, audiophile or cult (rather than mass-market) audio equipment

**Idler**  a rubber-tyred drive wheel in a turntable or tape deck

**MIDI**  Musical Instrument Digital Interface - system for linking synthesizers and keyboards so that music can be created, recorded, and played back under the control of a computer "sequencer".

**Monitor**  a high-quality loudspeaker originally used for studio monitoring. Or, of a tape system, a means of listening to a recording as it is being made

**Moving-coil loudspeaker**  the most common type of drive unit, in which a vibrating cone produces the sound; a coil attached to the cone and surrounded by a magnet is fed with the output from the amplifier

**MP3**  a computer software application for compressing a digital recording so that it takes up less space in, for example, computer memory

**Noise**  in audio, any unwanted signal that spoils the sound, such as tape hiss (which can be lessened by a noise reduction system such as Dolby), or rumble from a turntable motor

**Pick-up (head)**  term loosely used to mean a tone-arm and/or the cartridge fitted to it

**Platter**  term sometimes used for the rotating part of a turntable (which can also mean just that) or record deck

**Pre-amplifier**  the first stage of amplification, including selection and matching with source components. There may also be tone controls, filters, and other facilities, when it may instead be called a control unit.

**Printed circuit**  system introduced in the mid 1950s whereby an etched copper layer on an insulating panel replaced most hand-wiring of components

**RDS**  Radio Data System - system for transmitting extra text or audio information on FM

**Receiver**  a combination of a hi-fi tuner and amplifier, although the term is sometimes used to describe any radio receiver

**Ribbon loudspeaker**  a type of loudspeaker in which the sound is produced by an aluminium or similar ribbon vibrating in a magnetic field when the amplifier output is fed to it

**Rumble**  low-frequency mechanical noise from a turntable motor, audible through speakers

**SA-CD**  Super-Audio CD, a new format offering multi-channel sound and better quality than ordinary CDs

**Signal**  in audio, widely used to mean an electrical current or voltage that represents the wanted sound. A good "signal-to-noise ratio" means that unwanted noise (hiss, for example) is very low

**Solid-state**  term used to describe a system in which transistors or integrated circuits are used rather than tubes

**Stroboscope**  device for checking turntable speed accuracy

**Stylus**  the diamond (or sapphire, in cheap record players) tip that tracks the record groove

**Sub-woofer**  a loudspeaker that reproduces deep bass frequencies

**Tone-arm (or pick-up arm)**  one chosen and fitted to a turntable unit, or already provided on an integrated record deck, which carries the cartridge

**Tracking**  the following of the record groove by the stylus. "Tracking error" is caused by the difference between the straight path followed by the master record cutter and the arc swept by a normal pivoted tone-arm

**Transcription**  a high-quality turntable (originally, a turntable used in broadcasting to transcribe radio programmes to disc)

**Tube**  shorthand for "vacuum tube", a glass device containing two, three, or more electrodes. This was the key element of radio and amplifying equipment until transistors were developed. A triode is an early type of tube now enjoying new acclaim in high-end hi-fi

**Tweeter**  drive unit for high (treble) frequencies

**Valve**  mainly British term for tube

**Watt**  unit of power, used, for example, to indicate the output of an amplifier

**Woofer**  drive unit for low (bass) frequencies

**Wow and flutter**  slow and fast variations in musical pitch caused by unstable speed of a turntable or tape deck

There are dealers all over the world who buy and sell audio equipment such as the items featured in this book. Some deal in vintage radios or hi-fi, while others specialize in classic '50s, '60s, or '70s design, which may include radios and record players. Collectible hi-fi items in good original condition from names such as Quad, McIntosh, Thorens, or Bang & Olufsen often fetch high prices, but less famous marques can be much cheaper. If you want to sell equipment, try not to build up your hopes too much: much mass-market audio equipment of the past thirty years or so is often worth very little.

Where you should buy depends on your technical knowledge and practical skills, and on whether you want to buy a nearly mint item or whether you want to buy a "wreck" to restore yourself. Some dealers offer a repair and restoration service, or sell spare parts.

Many vintage audio dealers are small operators trading through the Internet or by mail rather than a through a store, and the Internet is much the best way to track down someone who has what you are looking for, although the classified advertisements in some hi-fi magazines are worth a look. Local "swap-meet" sales and on-line auctions like e-Bay are also an increasingly popular way of buying and selling classic audio equipment. The Internet is also a good place to track down technical data and a way of finding collectors' clubs and museums in your area.

www.agtannenbaum.com  manuals and data for sale

www.antiqueradio.com  print magazine, links, and classifieds

www.antiqueradios.com  resources directory, and classifieds (different site to the one above)

www.audioclassics.com  hi-fi equipment, books, and manuals bought and sold

www.audiogon.com  high-end sales and auctions

www.audioreview.it  Italian high-end audio magazine

www.audiotools.com  details of hi-fi companies past and present and links to more information

www.audioweb.com  large directory of resources, classifieds, discussion forums, etc

www.bassboy.com.au/getreel  site focusing on open-reel tape recorders

www.deadwaxcafe.com  information and classifieds for vinyl and vinyl equipment

www.designaddict.com  includes directory of vintage design dealers

www.enjoythemusic.com  portal for online high-end and classic hi-fi magazines

www.4music.net  equipment classifieds

www.hifichoice.co.uk  includes archive of equipment reviews

www.hifiheaven.com  directory of audio resources and classifieds

www.mauritron.co.uk  audio servicing data

www.oldradioworld.de  radio gallery and resources directory

www.orionbluebook.com  equipment valuation service

www.stereophile.com  online archive of long-standing US magazine

www.stereosound.co.jp  Japanese high-end magazine

www.techwiz.com  technical manuals and data for sale

www.vacuumtube.com  online version of US "Vacuum Tube Valley" print magazine, plus restoration, servicing, and sales

www.vintageradio.com  radio-servicing data

www.worldtubeaudio.com  directory and links

# index

# acknowledgements

## AUTHOR'S ACKNOWLEDGEMENTS

Many people provided advice, information or original material while this book was being put together. The author would like to thank the following: Andy Arthurs, John Bamford, Mike Barker, Alan Bednall, Ger Bruens, Roy Brooker, Gerd Clasen, Roy Coulthurst, Robin Day, Edward Dunstall, Barry Fox, Andrew Fowler, David Fowler, Keith Geddes, Kenneth Grange, John Grant, Phil Green, Peter Harries, Steve Harris, Andrew Harrison, Jonathan Hill, John Howes, Tom Karen, Ken Kessler, Charles Kittleson, Andy Linehan, Gordon Madgwick, Bob Marriott, Don McRitchie, Robert Monkovich, Terry O'Sullivan, Penny Sparke, Steven Rochlin, Geoff Rosenberg, Richard Seymour, Matt Sommers, Stephen Spicer, Paul Stenning, Gerald Wells, and all at Mitchell Beazley.

## PHOTOGRAPHIC CREDITS

Mitchell Beazley would like to acknowledge and thank the following companies and individuals for providing images for use in this book. We would especially like to thank Hi-Fi News magazine for their kind help in supplying photographs.

Key: **t** top, **b** bottom, **l** left, **r** right

**2** Glas Platz; **5** Enrico Tedeschi; **7** Unison Research; **8** Wilson Benesch; **12** V&A Picture Library; **13t** Advertising Archives, **b** Henry Blackham; **14t** The British Library, **b** Enrico Tedeschi; **15** David Attwood; **18** Advertising Archives; **19** Pictorial Press; **20** Advertising Archives; **21t** Hulton Archive; **22r** Robert Opie Collection; **23** Advertising Archives; **24** Robert Opie Collection; **25t** Herman Miller, Inc/Dale Rooks, **b** Hi-Fi News; **26** Advertising Archives; **27t** Science & Society Picture Library, **b** Revox GmBH; **28t** Steve Spicer, Kiewa Valley Audio; **29** The British Library. **30** The British Library/The National Sound Archive; **31l** Redferns/Michael Ochs Archive, **r** The Gramophone; **32** Hi-Fi News; **33t** The British Library, courtesy Harman Kardon, **b** Marantz Hi-Fi UK; **34** Quad Electroacoustics; **35t** Hi Fi News, **b** Thorens Export company; **37t** Hi-Fi News; **38** Klipsch Europe; **39b** Hi-Fi News; **40t** Lansing Heritage Website www.audioheritage.org/Harman International; **41** Hi-Fi News; **42** Octopus Publishing Group/Tim Ridley; **44** Enrico Tedeschi; **45b** Enrico Tedeschi; **46** David Attwood; **47** Sotheby's Picture Library; **48** Redferns/Michael Ochs Archive; **49t** Corbis/Ted Spiegel, **b** Redferns; **50** Robin Day; **51b** Giles Chapman Library; **52b** Octopus Publishing Group/Tim Ridley/Boom!; **53t** Advertising Archives, **54** Enrico Tedeschi; **55t** Hi-Fi News, **b** Octopus Publishing Group/Tim Ridley/Twenty Twenty One; **56**, **57** Hi-Fi News; **58** Lansing Heritage Website www.audioheritage.org/Harman International; **59**, **61**, **62**, **63t** Hi-Fi News; **63b** SME Ltd; **64** Octopus Publishing Group/Tim Ridley/Boom!; **65** Thorens Export company; **66** Philips International BV; **67t** Advertising Archives, **b** Octopus Publishing Group/Tim Ridley/Boom!; **68** Octopus Publishing Group/Steve Tanner; **71t** John Howes, **b** Gordon Madgwick; **72** Kenneth Grange; **73t** Hi-Fi News, **b** Linn Products Ltd; **74tl** & **r** Madrigal Audio Laboratories, Inc, **b** Naim Audio Ltd; **75** Hi-Fi News; **77t** EMS, **b** Redferns/Outline; **78** Enrico Tedeschi; **79t** V&A Picture Library, **b** Phil Green; **80** Hi-Fi News; **81** Kenneth Grange; **82**, **83**, **84** Hi-Fi News; **85t** Advertising Archives, **b** Hi-Fi News; **86tl** David Fowler; **87l** Redferns/Richie Aaron, **r** Corbis/Roger Ressmeyer; **88** Audio Classics; **89t** Sotheby's Picture Library; **90** Nagra Kudelski (GB); **91** Advertising Archives; **92**, **93t** Hi-Fi News, **93b** Phil Green; **94t** Hi-Fi News, **b** Roger Dixon; **96** Design Museum, Delft University of Technology; **97t** Advertising Archives, **b** Christie's Images; **98** Enrico Tedeschi; **100t** Philips International BV, **b** Sony United Kingdom Limited; **101**, **102** Hi-Fi News; **103** Schneider Electronics AG; **104** Redferns/Nicky J Sims; **105t** Redferns/Ebet Roberts; **106**, **107** Hi-Fi News; **108** Krell Industries, Inc; **109t** Nakamichi Europe, **b** Pioneer GB Ltd; **110** Hi-Fi News; **111t** Wilson Audio Specialities Inc, **111b**, **112** Hi-Fi News; **113l** Corbis, **r** Redferns/Mick Hutson; **114-18** Hi-Fi News; **119t** John Howes, **b** Hi-Fi News **121l** Rex Features/Sipa, **121r**, **122t** Hi-Fi News, **122b** Sony United Kingdom Limited; **123** Enrico Tedeschi; **124** Philips International BV; **125t** Ron Arad Associates; **126** Hi-Fi News; **128** Wadia; **129** Hi-Fi News/Panasonic; **130** Marantz Hi-Fi UK; **131t** Pioneer GB Ltd, **b** TAG McLaren; **132** Sony United Kingdom Limited; **133t** Kenwood UK, **133b** Musical Fidelity; **134** Apple Macintosh; **135t** Redferns, **b** Wall of Sound Recordings Ltd; **136** Avid; **137t** Synthesis, **b** Jadis; **138** Oracle Audio Technologies Inc; **139t** Cardas Audio Ltd, **b** Hi-Fi News; **140t** Avantgarde Acoustic GmbH, **b** Blueroom Loudspeakers Ltd; **141** O'hEocha Design UK and Ireland; **142l** B & W Loudspeakers Ltd, **r** Carfrae Loudspeakers; **143l** Absolute Sounds, **r** MartinLogan Ltd; **145t** KEF; **146** Hi-Fi News; **147** Nakamichi Europe; **148** Officina Alessi; **149t** Psion Infomedia Ltd, **b** Lexon; **150** Rio Inc; **151t** Philips International BV, **b** Robert Bosch Ltd; **152** Aiwa UK; **153t** JVC (UK) Ltd, **b** Nokia.

U.W.E.L. LEARNING RESOURCES